Last-Minute SCIENCE FAIR PROJECTS

Last-Minute
SCIENCE FAIR
PROJECTS

WHEN YOUR BUNSEN'S NOT BURNING
BUT THE CLOCK'S REALLY TICKING

By Sudipta Bardhan-Quallen

STERLING

New York / London
www.sterlingpublishing.com

Photography by Steve Hutchings, Michael Hnatov.
Illustrations by Janet Pietrobono.
Book design by Ellen Lynch.

Library of Congress Cataloging-in-Publication Data

Bardhan-Quallen, Sudipta.
  Last-minute science fair projects : when your Bunsen's not burning but the clock's really ticking / Sudipta Bardhan-Quallen.
     p. cm.
  Includes index.
  ISBN-13: 978-1-4027-1690-4
  ISBN-10: 1-4027-1690-7
  1. Science projects—Juvenile literature. I. Title.
  Q182.3.B367 2006
  507.8—dc22

                                    2005034455

10 9 8 7 6 5 4 3 2

Published by Sterling Publishing Co., Inc.
387 Park Avenue South, New York, NY 10016
© 2006 by Sudipta Bardhan-Quallen
Distributed in Canada by Sterling Publishing
c/o Canadian Manda Group, 165 Dufferin Street
Toronto, Ontario, Canada M6K 3H6
Distributed in the United Kingdom by GMC Distribution Services
Castle Place, 166 High Street, Lewes, East Sussex, England BN7 1XU
Distributed in Australia by Capricorn Link (Australia) Pty. Ltd.
P.O. Box 704, Windsor, NSW 2756, Australia

Printed in China
All rights reserved

Sterling ISBN-13: 978-1-4027-5315-2
        ISBN-10: 1-4027-5315-2

Contents

Introduction

One morning, your science teacher writes an announcement on the blackboard: ☞

Oh, no! you think. I haven't had a chance to start!

Or maybe, I don't know where to begin!

Or even, I completely forgot about the whole science fair thing!

Face it, between soccer practice and piano lessons and English homework (or was it tennis practice and flute lessons and math homework?), you've hardly had any time to spend on a science fair project. What are you going to do?

Maybe you're really responsible (and soccer practice was cancelled because of rain), and you get to work right after the first reminder. Or maybe you got busy again with drama rehearsals and, all of a sudden, some more days have passed, and your teacher is writing:

Now I'm really in trouble, you think. How could I do a great science fair experiment in a week, never mind in just a day?

Luckily, you bought this book. In these pages, you'll find project after project that will be sure to wow the crowd and the science fair judges. Whether you have a week, a weekend, or even just a day, you'll be able to find a terrific project to do.

But you should probably get started now!

Science All Around You

Since you're working at the last minute, you need to find your materials quickly. Fortunately, many of the things you'll need for the experiments in this book can be found around the house. For example, your kitchen is a treasure trove of science goodies. Many experiments will use things such as lemon juice, vinegar, baking soda, vegetable oil, food coloring, table salt, sugar, dish soap, yeast, and all sorts of food—raisins, apples, oranges, milk, potatoes, and even chicken bones.

When you're done raiding your kitchen, check out your bathroom (and while you're at it, check out your mother's bathroom). You'll be set if you find a hair dryer, soap, rubbing alcohol, nail polish remover, iodine, petroleum jelly, and your mother's wrinkle cream (if she needs wrinkle cream, that is).

The next stops will be the garage and the backyard. You can do a lot of science with the things you find in these places. Look for old pipes (your parents may be able to help you figure out what the pipes are made of), lightbulbs, leaves, grass, and dirt, of course.

Depending on the experiment you choose, you might find that one or two of the materials aren't already in your house. Don't worry—almost everything can be found easily at a supermarket, hardware store, garden supply store, or science supply store. In most cases, one trip should be enough to gather all the materials.

Pick the Perfect Project

The projects in this book are separated into three sections, based on how long it will take to complete the experiments. It is very important that you choose a project that you will be able to finish! Read all the instructions ahead of time to make sure you understand everything before you get started. This will help things go smoothly.

It is also important that you choose a topic that interests you. You'll have much more fun if you find the topic exciting. Remember—although science fairs are about learning, they are also about having fun.

The Project and the Presentation

After you've selected a project, gather all the materials you'll need. Make sure you have a notebook and pencil handy to write down everything you do and all your observations. Try to answer all the questions about the project in this book, and if you think of more questions yourself, make a note of them in your notebook.

Even though you will follow the instructions in this book, it is important to write down what you do in your own words as you do the experiment. This way, if you get a different result than you expected, you can go back and make sure the reason isn't because you did something differently.

Many science fairs require that you do a presentation of your project for the judges. As you record your observations, think about how you can present your results to your science fair audience. Should you take photographs? Should you be making sketches? Should you repeat the experiment at the science fair during your presentation? If you keep these things in mind, you'll be much more prepared for the presentation— the last thing you need at the last minute is to have to redo the experiment because you didn't take pictures the first time around!

The Project Report

Another common requirement at science fairs is a project report. There are different ways to write these reports, but one good approach is to incorporate the following things:

✓ **Introduction:** In this section, cover background information about your project. Describe why you found the project interesting and why you wanted to do it.

✓ **Hypothesis:** This is a sentence or two that describes what you expect to see as a result of the experiment. There are sample hypothesis statements provided with each experiment in this book.

✓ **Materials:** This is a list of everything used for your project. Make a note of amounts, weights, and volumes when appropriate (which means you say "1 cup of vinegar" instead of "some vinegar").

✓ **Procedures:** This section should describe everything you did during the experiment. Make sure you record which steps you were able to do alone and which ones required an adult's help.

✓ **Results:** In this section, you should list what observations you recorded and what results you saw. Discuss whether or not you proved your hypothesis. Include any problems you encountered during the experiment and how they may have affected your results.

✓ **Bibliography:** This section lists all the sources you used to do your project and write your report.

Be On Time... Next Year

As you look through this book, hopefully you'll find a few projects that seem interesting. Although you have to choose one to do this year (and choose quickly—the clock is ticking!), you should also think ahead to next year. If something seems appealing, go ahead and get started!

Each experiment has two extension activities attached to it. While you're rushing, you may not have time to do these. But if you start early, your next science fair project can incorporate the main activity and both the extension activities— which is sure to impress the judges.

A WEEK OR TWO

Light and Dark

When you try to grow a plant, you usually give it plenty of water and plenty of sunlight. But have you ever wondered what happens if a plant doesn't get sunlight—or any light at all?

In general, light is very important to the life of a plant. Without light, plants can't make a lot of *chlorophyll,* the chemical that gives them their green color. Light is so important, in fact, that most plants exhibit a behavior called *phototropism*—that is, they grow toward a source of light. Even a faint light source, such as the little bit of light that comes through under the door inside a dark closet, is enough to make plants stretch and grow, just to try to reach it. This leads to a very different growth pattern from plants grown in sunlight.

5. Every other day, measure how tall each of the plants has grown.

6. Observe the plants for at least fourteen days, but feel free to continue the experiment longer.

Key words
- Chlorophyll
- Phototropism

Question
Do plants grow differently in the dark than they do in sunlight?

Hypothesis
Plants left to grow in the dark will be less green and will grow longer and thinner than plants left in sunlight.

Materials
- 10 small bean plants (grow these using the instructions in "Bean Sprouts," next page), planted one to a pot or cup
- A sunlit windowsill
- A dark closet or basement
- A ruler
- A camera (optional)

Procedure

1. Label the plants 1 through 10 and measure their heights. Record their appearance, and if you want, take a photograph of the way they look before you begin the experiment.

2. Place five plants on the sunlit windowsill.

3. Place the other five plants in the dark closet or basement.

4. Water the plants once a day, making sure the soil stays moist. When you water them, record any changes in their general appearance.

Results

Did the plants in the closet continue to grow? Were they different in appearance from the plants left in sunlight? Did the plants in the closet look stretched out and longer, as if they were reaching for something?

Display Tip

Display one plant that grew in sunlight and one plant that grew in the closet. Point out the differences in the way the plants grew.

Extension Question

Do the plants from the closet change back to a more "normal" appearance if you let them grow in sunlight again?

Extension Question

How long can plants survive in the dark? Extend the experiment to last for a month instead of two weeks. Do any of the plants die? Or do they keep growing taller and thinner?

Bean Sprouts

To grow bean sprouts, all you need are a few dozen beans (pinto beans or lima beans work well), some water, a couple of paper towels, a cup, and some time. In a cup of water, soak two or three dozen beans overnight. In the morning, drain the water and spread the beans on a paper towel. Place another paper towel in a cup and moisten it with water. Then gather the beans that were spread on the first paper towel and place them in the cup, paper towel and all.

Leave the cup on a sunny windowsill and make sure the paper towels are moistened every day. Within a week, you should see bean sprouts, which can be planted in potting soil.

Stop Rot

From time to time, someone leaves food around the house too long and it spoils. Some foods, however, spoil more quickly, while others seem to last longer. Often foods that have been treated with *preservatives* can stay fresh for very long periods of time. Preservatives can be artificial chemicals developed by scientists, or they can be natural substances found all over the place—including your kitchen.

Key word
Preservatives

Question
Are there things around the house that can act as preservatives?

Hypothesis
Some household items can help prevent food from rotting.

Materials
- 1 apple, sliced into six equally sized pieces
- 6 small jars, each large enough to fit an apple piece
- Enough of the following substances to fill 1 jar each:
    Salt
    Sugar
    Antibacterial hand soap
    Vinegar
    Water
- A permanent marker
- Several paper plates
- Several disposable utensils

Safety Warning
At the end of this experiment, have an adult properly dispose of the food, since it may be rotting.

Procedure

1. Use the marker to label the six jars, as follows "Control," "Salt," "Sugar," "Antibacterial Soap," "Vinegar," and "Water."

2. Place an apple piece inside each jar.

3. Completely cover the apple pieces in the substance you wrote on the label (for example, pour enough salt into the jar labeled "salt" to submerge the apple piece). Do not put anything other than the apple piece into the jar marked "Control."

4. Set all the jars in a cool, dry place.

5. After one week, retrieve the jars. Examine the apple pieces and record any changes in their appearance. To examine the pieces covered in salt, sugar, or anything else you cannot see through easily, dump the contents of the jar onto a paper plate and then use the disposable utensils to "dig" for the apple piece.

Results

Which apple pieces rotted? Which pieces seemed to be preserved? Did the preserved pieces seem dried out? Did you notice any color changes? Any changes in the texture of the apples?

Display Tip

Take photographs of the different apple pieces at the beginning and end of the experiment. Display the photos to show the effects of preservatives.

Extension Question

You may have found that some of the household items can act as preservatives. Now, try to find out how long the effect lasts. Repeat this experiment, and at the end, take the apple pieces out of the jars and put them in new, empty jars. Make sure you label which piece has been in contact with what substance. Set the jars in a cool, dry place and examine them after one week. Do you see any rot now?

Extension Question

Examine with a magnifying glass any mold that grew on the apple pieces. Does all the mold look the same? Did some of the test preservatives prevent one type of mold but not another?

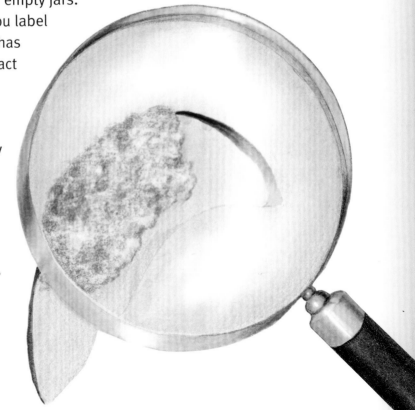

Sprouting Seeds

The first step a plant takes in growing from a seed into a seedling is called *germination*—when the plant embryo contained in the seed sprouts and begins to grow. Seeds require certain things in order to germinate—and one of the most important things is moisture. But is water the best liquid for seeds? Try germinating beans in different liquids to see if you can figure out what seeds like best.

Key words
- Germination
- Embryo

Question
What liquids best help a seed to sprout and grow?

Hypothesis
The properties of a liquid (acidity, sugar concentration, etc.) will affect the rate at which a seed sprouts.

Materials
- 7 small plastic bags (1 for each liquid sample)
- 7 paper towels (1 for each liquid sample)
- Enough of the following liquids to moisten 1 paper towel each:
    Water
    Baby oil
    Vinegar
    Dish soap (2 tablespoons [30 mL] of liquid soap dissolved in 1 cup [240 mL] of water)
    Sugar water (2 tablespoons [30 mL] of sugar dissolved in 1 cup [240 mL] of water)
    Salt water (2 tablespoons [30 mL] of salt dissolved in 1 cup [240 mL] of water)
    Rubbing alcohol
- 21 pre-soaked beans (beans should be soaked in tap water overnight)

Safety Warning
Be careful when handling a chemical such as alcohol, since it is flammable.

Procedure
1. Label each of the plastic bags with the liquid sample names.

2. Fold the paper towels and place one in each plastic bag.

3. Moisten the paper towels with the appropriate liquid.

4. Place three pre-soaked beans in each plastic bag.

5. Place the plastic bags in a sunny place. Examine the paper towels every day and re-moisten them with the appropriate liquids when necessary.

6. Examine the seeds every other day for two weeks, recording any changes in their appearance.

Results

Under which conditions did seeds sprout? Which seeds sprouted most quickly? Which seeds did not sprout at all? Did the seeds that did not sprout look the same as when you began the experiment?

Display Tip

Take photographs of the seeds when you examine them. Display the photographs during your presentation.

Extension Question

Do the different liquids have the same effect on seedlings as they do on seeds? Repeat this experiment using young bean plants instead of seeds. What effects do you see?

Extension Question

How much moisture is best for germinating seeds? For each liquid sample, set up two paper cups with three pre-soaked beans in each. Add enough liquid to just cover the beans in one cup, and completely submerge the beans in the other cup. Which seeds sprout first?

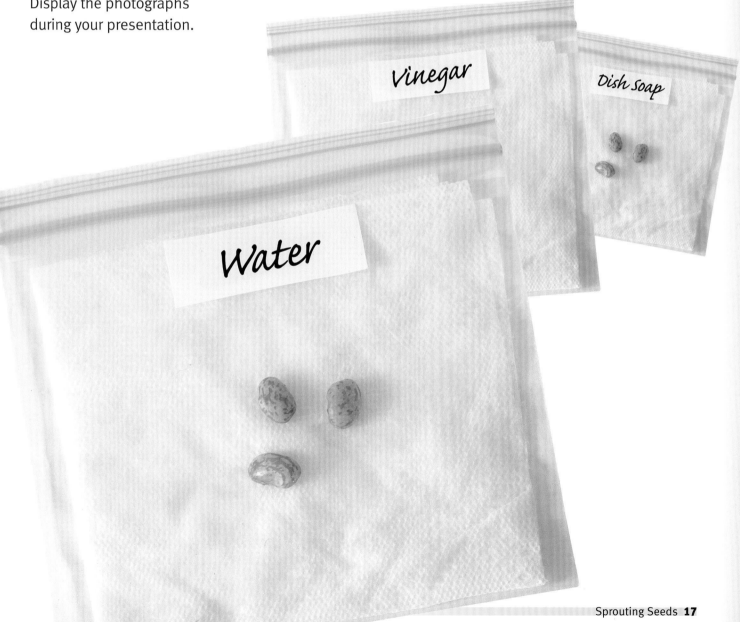

Get Ripe

Have you ever heard the expression, "One bad apple ruins the whole barrel"? Bad apples—ones that are overripe or have cut or punctured skin, for example—can make other fruit ripen more quickly. But what makes this happen? One explanation is that spoiled or damaged fruit gives off some kind of gas that ripens other fruit. Test that theory with this experiment!

The gas is called *ethylene*, which can help ripen a whole variety of fruit, including tomatoes, bananas, citrus, pineapples, dates, persimmons, pears, apples, melons, mangos, avocados, papayas, and even jujubes!

Key words
- Ripening
- Ethylene

Question
Can the gas produced by a ripe apple cause another type of fruit to ripen?

Hypothesis
The gas produced by ripe fruit is the same across different types of fruit; therefore, a ripe apple is able to promote the ripening of a banana or tomato.

Materials
- 3 ripe apples
- 3 green bananas
- 3 green tomatoes
- 3 firm mangoes
- 6 large plastic bags
- Tape (as needed to seal plastic bags)

Procedure
1. Just to be sure that the ripe apples will produce a lot of gas, nick their skins in a few places with a fork or knife (you may want an adult's help for this).

2. Place an apple in each of three plastic bags.

3. Place one green banana, one green tomato, and one firm mango in the bags with the apples, so that each of the three bags contains an apple and one other fruit.

4. Place one green banana, one green tomato, or one firm mango in each of the three remaining bags.

5. Seal the plastic bags well, using tape if necessary.

6. Place the bags where they will not be disturbed and where they are not in direct sunlight.

7. Place the remaining three unripe fruits in the same place as the bags.

8. Every day for two weeks, examine all the fruit. Record any changes in color, texture, or firmness you observe.

Results
Did the unripe fruits in the bags with the ripe apples ripen most quickly? Did the unripe fruits in the bags by themselves ripen more quickly than the fruits left out?

Display Tip
Take photographs of the fruits over time so you can show your audience how much they changed throughout the course of the experiment.

Extension Question
Does ethylene gas linger in the refrigerator? Let two or three ripe apples sit in a crisper compartment of your fridge. After a week, remove the apples and put a green banana in the crisper. Place another green banana in the fridge in a separate area. Which of the bananas ripens faster?

Extension Question
Do fruits produce higher quantities of ethylene gas over time? Place a ripe apple and a fresh apple together in a sealed plastic bag. After one week, place each of these apples in new plastic bag and add a fresh apple to each bag. Seal the bags. Which of the new apples ripens faster?

Plant Power Sources

Plants use sunlight to make energy to grow. They absorb sunlight and use it to break down *chlorophyll* (the chemical that gives plants their green color) during *photosynthesis*, the chemical reaction that leads to the production of energy. Photosynthesis occurs mainly in the plant's leaves, which are, in a way, the power sources for the whole plant. If a plant loses too many leaves, its growth may be slowed down.

Key words
- Chlorophyll
- Photosynthesis

Question
Do plants with more leaves grow faster than plants with fewer leaves?

Hypothesis
The more leaves a bean plant has, the taller it will grow.

Materials
- 9 small bean plants (grow plants using the instructions in "Bean Sprouts," page 13), planted one to a pot or cup
- A sunlit windowsill
- A ruler
- A camera (optional)

Procedure
1. Count the leaves on each plant and determine what the lowest number of leaves on a plant is. Call this number the "maximum."

2. On the first three plants, remove leaves if necessary to leave them with the maximum number of leaves. Label these plants 1, 2, and 3, and measure their heights.

3. On the next three plants, remove leaves if necessary to leave them with the half the maximum number of leaves. Label these plants 4, 5, and 6, and measure their heights.

4. On the last three plants, remove all of the leaves. Label these plants 7, 8, and 9, and measure their heights.

5. If you want, take a photograph of how the plants look before you begin the experiment.

6. Water the plants once a day, making sure the soil stays moist. When you water them, record any changes in their general appearance.

7. Every other day, measure how tall each of the plants has grown. Take photographs if you want.

8. Observe the plants for at least fourteen days, but feel free to continue the experiment longer.

Results

Which plants grew the tallest? Did the plants with the greatest number of leaves grow the most? Which plants appeared healthier in general? Did the plants with all their leaves removed eventually grow more leaves?

Extension Question

Is there the same effect on growth when the leaves are blocked from sunlight but left on the plant? Repeat this experiment, but instead of removing leaves, cover them up with aluminum foil.

Extension Question

Does it make a difference to the growth of the plant whether you remove younger, newly formed leaves or older, lower leaves? What is more important to the growth of the plant—the total number of leaves left or the kind of leaves left to grow?

Display Tip

Bring the surviving plants to the science fair to display them to your audience. Also, display any photographs you took to show people how the plants changed. Make a graph of the height of each plant over time to display at the science fair as well.

Oooh!

Fungus Garden

There are microorganisms called *fungi* all around us all the time. Most of the time, fungi are microscopic and we can't see that they are there. But sometimes, such as when food rots, a fungus can grow large enough for people to see with their naked eyes. This happens because the fungus keeps reproducing on the rotting food—when enough individual *microbes* gather together in one place, we are able to see a fuzzy, sticky, or slimy mold!

There are many different types of fungi—see how many you can grow in a fungus garden made from a jar and your favorite foods.

Key words
- Fungus
- Microbes
- Desiccant

Question
Can we watch fungi grow?

Hypothesis
If left undisturbed inside a jar, the fungi on foods will grow as the food rots to create a colorful fungus garden.

Materials
- An empty and clean mayonnaise jar with a lid
- Several food samples, such as pieces of bread, apple, cucumber, or cheese
- Enough water to moisten food samples

Safety Warning
At the end of this experiment, have an adult properly dispose of the food since it will be covered in fungus.

Procedure
1. Place the food inside the jar. Don't overfill the jar, but try to have a few different kinds of food.

2. Sprinkle a few teaspoons of water into the jar to moisten everything.

3. Close the lid and leave the jar on a countertop or table where it won't be disturbed. Also, place it in an area that is out of direct sunlight.

4. Observe any changes to the food inside the fungus garden every other day for two weeks. Record your observations.

5. Do not open the fungus garden throughout the experiment. When the experiment is over, ask an adult to dispose of the fungus garden.

Results

How long did it take for the first fungus to grow? How many different types of fungi did you see? Did more than one type of fungus grow on any one type of food? Did the fungi seem to spread over time? Did the foods change in shape or texture as the fungi grew?

Display Tip

Because fungi can be harmful in large quantities, do not bring your fungus garden to the science fair. Instead, take photographs of your fungus garden over time to display during the science fair. Also, take close-up photographs of the different types of fungi you see.

Extension Question

Do different fungi grow in the dark versus in sunlight? Set up two fungus gardens with exactly the same foods, but leave one in sunlight and one in a dark basement or closet. Compare the fungus gardens after two weeks.

Extension Question

How important is moisture to fungus growth? Set up three fungus gardens with exactly the same foods. Add a sprinkling of water to the first, add no water to the second, and add 1 cup (240 mL) of salt (a desiccant—something that absorbs moisture to keep things dry) to the last. Compare the fungus gardens after two weeks.

Picky Eaters

Birds in your neighborhood may seem as if they're always looking for a free meal, but the truth is that birds can be very picky. See if your neighborhood birds have food preferences with this experiment.

Question

Do birds prefer one type of food over another? Do different types of birds prefer different foods?

Hypothesis

Birds, like humans, have preferences over the types of foods they like to eat.

Materials

- 4 plastic disposable plates
- Tape
- Several heavy washers, to tape to the bottoms of the plates to keep them stable
- A kitchen scale
- 1 container of each of the following foods:
    - Sunflower seeds
    - Canary seeds
    - Artificial suet (available at pet supply stores)
    - Peanut butter
- Access to a spot outdoors that can be observed from a distance (a balcony or deck would work well, or a spot in the park a few feet [meters] from a bench)

Procedure

1. Tape some washers to the bottoms of the plastic disposable plates, making sure the plates still lie flat.

2. Using the kitchen scale, measure out 3 ounces (85 g) of each type of food. Put the food on the plates, one type per plate.

3. Place the plates in the outdoor spot you've selected. Find a place where you can observe the birds that come to eat without scaring them away.

4. For the next hour, keep track of the number of birds that visit and which kinds of food they eat. Also keep track of any environmental things that may affect the birds' feeding (like a fire engine siren or a prowling cat, which may scare birds away).

5. After an hour, retrieve the plates. Weigh each type of food to determine how much is left.

6. Repeat this experiment at the same time of day every day for a week.

Results

Did each variety of bird have a favorite food? Were there any foods that were eaten by all birds in the experiment? Did the type of food a bird ate seem to be related to the bird's beak shape? Did more birds visit as the week continued?

Extension Question

How do the results of this experiment change if you use a tube feeder or other type of bird feeder? Do you think the type of feeder affects the varieties of birds that visit or how much they eat?

Display Tip

Take many photographs of the birds eating during the experiment. This will also help you identify the types of birds. You could also graph the number of birds that visit each day and the amount of each type of food that is eaten each day.

Extension Question

How do the results of this experiment change if you set it up at a different time of day? Do some birds prefer to eat in the morning? Do others prefer to eat at night?

Orange Mummy

When you think of a mummy, you probably think of ancient Egypt and pharaohs buried in golden sarcophagi. In reality, mummies have been found in countries all over the world, including Peru, Mexico, and China. The process of *mummification* involves removing all the water from living tissues. In Egypt, burial workers would use *natron*, a natural salt, to dry out the body, and then they would wrap the body in bandages.

You can try to mummify something at home. You may not have natron, but there are plenty of other household *desiccants* that can be used to dry out living tissues—such as those in an orange.

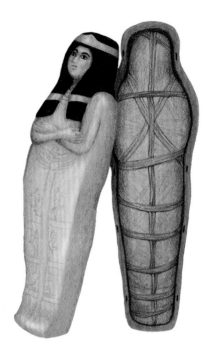

Key words
- Mummification
- Natron
- Desiccant

Question
Can you make a mummy out of an orange?

Hypothesis
By using a desiccant like baking soda, you can dry out an orange enough to preserve it like a mummy.

Materials
- A kitchen scale
- 2 oranges
- 2 large mayonnaise jars, cleaned and dried, with lids (make sure these are large enough to fit an apple)
- Enough baking soda to fill one of the jars

Safety Warning
At the end of this experiment, have an adult properly dispose of the oranges, since they may be rotting.

Procedure
1. Weigh both oranges—remember which is which!

2. Add about an inch (2.5 cm) of baking soda to one of the mayonnaise jars. Drop in one orange over the baking soda. Cover the orange with more baking soda, completely filling the jar.

3. Place the second orange in the other empty jar.

4. Replace the lids on both jars and place them in a cool, dry place in the shade.

5. After seven days, examine and weigh both oranges. Record any changes in weight, texture, or appearance.

6. Replace the oranges in the jars as they were before (bury the first orange in the baking soda again).

7. After another seven days, examine and weigh both oranges again, and record any observations.

Results

What happened to the baking soda–covered orange? Did it become dry and leathery? Did it get soft? How about the other orange that was just left in the jar—how did it compare to the baking soda–covered orange? Did one orange appear to be rotting? Were there any changes in smell between the two oranges?

Display Tip

If you continue mummifying the orange in baking soda, you may be able to display it at the science fair. To be on the safe side, display it inside a glass jar. Photographs will also help illustrate the differences between the mummified orange and the untreated orange.

Extension Question

Repeat this experiment using other desiccants, such as table salt or Epsom salts. Which one works best?

Extension Question

Try mummifying an orange that has been peeled. Does that work as well? What purpose does the orange skin (or the substitute for Egyptian bandages) seem to serve in mummification?

Crystal Garden

We've all seen crystals before—salt crystals and sugar crystals, for example. Although crystals form in many ways, one good way to grow a large chain of crystals is to use a *supersaturated* solution of sugar.

If you've ever added sugar to a cup of iced tea, you know that after you add a certain amount, the sugar stops dissolving and is left sitting at the bottom of the cup. At the point when you've added so much sugar to the cup that no more dissolves, the sugar and water solution is *saturated*. If you were to heat the water, however, more sugar could be dissolved. By dissolving sugar in heated water, you can create a supersaturated solution. Supersaturated solutions crystallize well as the water evaporates.

Key words
- Crystal
- Supersaturated
- Saturated

Question
Can crystals be grown along a piece of string?

Hypothesis
A supersaturated solution of sugar will form sugar crystals along a piece of string over time.

Materials
- A paper clip
- A piece of string, about 8 inches (20 cm) long
- A glass jar
- A pencil
- A saucepan
- 1 cup (240 mL) of water
- 2 cups (480 mL) of sugar
- A wooden spoon for stirring
- An adult's help to heat the water and sugar on the stove

Procedure

1. Tie the paper clip to one end of the string.

2. Hang the string into the jar so that the paper clip hangs just above the bottom of the jar. Tie the other end of the string to the pencil at this length and remove the string from the jar.

3. Pour the water into the saucepan. With an adult's help, begin heating the water on the stove.

4. Add the sugar to the saucepan a cup at a time, stirring with the wooden spoon to dissolve the sugar.

5. Keep adding sugar, stirring patiently, until no more will dissolve.

6. Have an adult help you pour the supersaturated sugar solution into the jar, leaving about an inch (2.5 cm) of air at the top of the jar.

7. Let the paper clip end of the string drop into the supersaturated sugar solution. BE CAREFUL! The solution will still be very hot. Balance the pencil over the jar to keep the string steady.

8. Let the jar cool, and then place it somewhere it will not be disturbed. Examine it once a week for two weeks.

Results

What happened as the water evaporated? Did sugar crystals form on the string? Were the crystals bigger or smaller than regular granulated sugar?

Display Tip

Display your crystal garden at the science fair! Just make sure no fungus or mold is growing on it.

Extension Question

Try this experiment using salt instead of sugar. Do the crystals look the same?

Extension Question

Compare granulated sugar to powdered sugar. How are they different? Now repeat this experiment using powdered sugar instead of granulated sugar. What kind of crystals do you get?

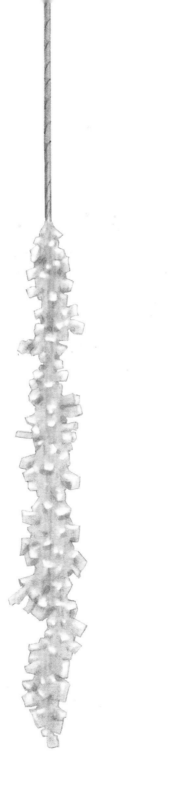

Build a Biosphere

A *biosphere* is a closed system that contains living and non-living components. It is completely self-sufficient—water, nutrients, oxygen, nitrogen, carbon dioxide, and everything else needed by the biosphere *organisms* are present. Everything is also recycled—for example, green plants in the biosphere use carbon dioxide and release oxygen, while some bacteria in the soil use oxygen and release carbon dioxide. These cycles maintain balance in the biosphere and keep life going. One good example of a completely self-sufficient biosphere is the planet Earth. You will build another in this experiment.

Key words
- Biosphere
- Organism

Question
Can you create a totally self-sufficient environment?

Hypothesis
A biosphere can be created using plants, bacteria (from soil), water, air, and different natural materials.

Materials
- A large mayonnaise jar with lid, cleaned and dried
- Enough pebbles to cover the bottom of the jar
- Enough horticultural charcoal (available at garden supply stores) to cover the pebbles
- A nylon stocking
- A pair of scissors
- A large mixing bowl
- Several spoons for mixing and assembly
- 1 cup (240 mL) of potting soil
- 1/2 cup (120 mL) of vermiculite (available at garden supply stores)
- 1/2 cup (120 mL) of peat moss
- 1/2 cup (120 mL) of compost
- 1/4 cup (60 mL) of aquarium sand
- 1 or 2 small plants
- Duct tape

Procedure

1. Sprinkle some pebbles into the mayonnaise jar, enough to create a thin layer at the bottom of the jar.

2. Sprinkle the horticultural charcoal over the pebbles to create a thin layer of charcoal.

3. Using the scissors, cut a circle from the nylon stocking to cover the charcoal layer and place it inside the jar.

4. In the bowl, mix the potting soil, vermiculite, peat moss, compost, and sand.

5. Spoon the mixture over the nylon stocking until you have a thin layer. Add some water so the mixture is moist.

6. Place the plant or plants inside the jar and sprinkle enough soil mixture to plant securely. Add more water so that everything is moist.

7. Screw the lid onto the jar. Seal the lid with the duct tape.

8. Place the biosphere somewhere in indirect sunlight. Observe it every day for at least two weeks. Try to see how long the biosphere survives.

Results

What happened to the biosphere over time? Did the plant continue to grow? Did the soil lose its moisture? Did you notice any changes in the color, texture, or moisture of the things inside?

Display Tip

Take a photograph of the biosphere every other day to show how it changes over time. You may also be able to display the biosphere during the science fair.

Extension Question

What would happen if you were to leave out one of the components of the biosphere? Repeat this experiment without one of the ingredients. Is the biosphere still self-sufficient?

Extension Question

How many plants can you put in the biosphere and still keep the system alive? Experiment to see how many plants it takes for resources to be used more quickly than they can be replaced.

A FEW SHORT DAYS

Sour Milk

Everyone knows that milk spoils if it is left out or if it is stored for too long. The reason for the spoilage is that bacteria and other microorganisms in the milk grow over time. These *microbes* grow faster at room temperature, which is why your parents always tell you to put the milk back in the refrigerator when you are done.

The microbes in milk are living things that need oxygen to survive. In this experiment, you will use a chemical called methylene blue as an indicator to tell you when the oxygen in the milk has been used up. When methylene blue is added to milk, it turns the milk blue, but this color disappears over time as the oxygen is used up by the microbes. The higher the concentration of microbes in the milk, the faster the blue color disappears.

Key words
- Microbes
- Methylene blue
- Bacteria
- Indicator

Question
How do temperature and time affect the growth of microbes in milk?

Hypothesis
Microbes in milk grow steadily over time, and they grow more quickly at room temperature than in the refrigerator.

Materials
- A measuring spoon
- A container of whole milk
- At least 5 clear plastic cups
- Plastic wrap
- A medicine dropper
- 1% methylene blue solution (available at science supply stores)

Safety Warning
Be careful when handling a chemical such as methylene blue, since direct contact can be harmful.

Procedure

1. This experiment requires you to leave samples of milk out at room temperature for different periods of time. It will be easiest if you coordinate the samples to be ready for the methylene blue test at the same time. For example, if you want to do your methylene blue test at 7:00 P.M. on Sunday, start setting up your samples on Saturday. You should test at least five time periods (milk left out for twenty-four, twelve, six, three, and zero hours), so the samples should be prepared at 7:00 P.M. Saturday, 7:00 A.M. Sunday, 1:00 P.M. Sunday, 4:00 P.M. Sunday, and 7:00 P.M. Sunday.

2. To prepare a sample, add 10 teaspoons (50 mL) of milk to a plastic cup and cover the top with the plastic wrap. Note the time the sample is prepared on the cup using the marker. Place the cup where it will not be disturbed and where it is out of direct sunlight.

3. Prepare at least five samples as described above.

4. When you prepare the "zero hours" sample, collect all the cups to perform the methylene blue test.

5. Record the time you start the methylene blue test.

6. Add three drops of the methylene blue solution to each cup and gently swirl it around. The milk should turn blue.

7. Examine the samples every six hours for the next two days. Record when each sample changes color from blue back to white.

Results

What happened to the color of the samples over time? Which samples changed color most quickly?

Display Tips

During the methylene blue tests, take photographs of the different samples when you examine them.

Extension Question

How does fat content affect the growth of microbes in milk? Repeat this experiment using nonfat milk, 1 percent milk, and whole milk. Which type of milk stays fresh longest?

Extension Question

How does contact with spoiled milk affect the rate of microbe growth in fresh milk? Repeat this experiment, adding a few drops of spoiled milk to one of the samples between steps 5 and 6. Do the colors change at the same rate as before?

Human Hair Hygrometer

Human hair is made of a protein called *keratin*, which is shaped like a coil. The coil can be stretched under certain circumstances—for example, when keratin gets wet, the coil unwinds and the strand of hair actually gets straighter and longer (think about your own hair after a shower). When the keratin in the hair dries again, the coil twists up again, making the length of the strand of hair shorter.

Because hair is able to change so dramatically when it is wet or dry, you can use a strand of hair to build a device called a *hygrometer*, which measures the humidity of the surroundings.

Key words

- Keratin
- Hygrometer

Question

Does humidity have an effect on the physical appearance of human hair?

Hypothesis

A strand of hair will lengthen or contract depending upon the humidity of the surroundings.

Materials

- 2 pieces of cardboard: one at least 2 inches (5 cm) long, the other at least 10 inches (25 cm) long
- A pair of scissors
- A penny
- A container of Superglue
- A long strand of hair least 8 inches (20 cm) long
- A pushpin
- A piece of Styrofoam about an inch square
- A pencil
- A hair dryer
- Adult supervision (to use the hair dryer)
- The news, a newspaper, or the Internet (to check the day's humidity level)

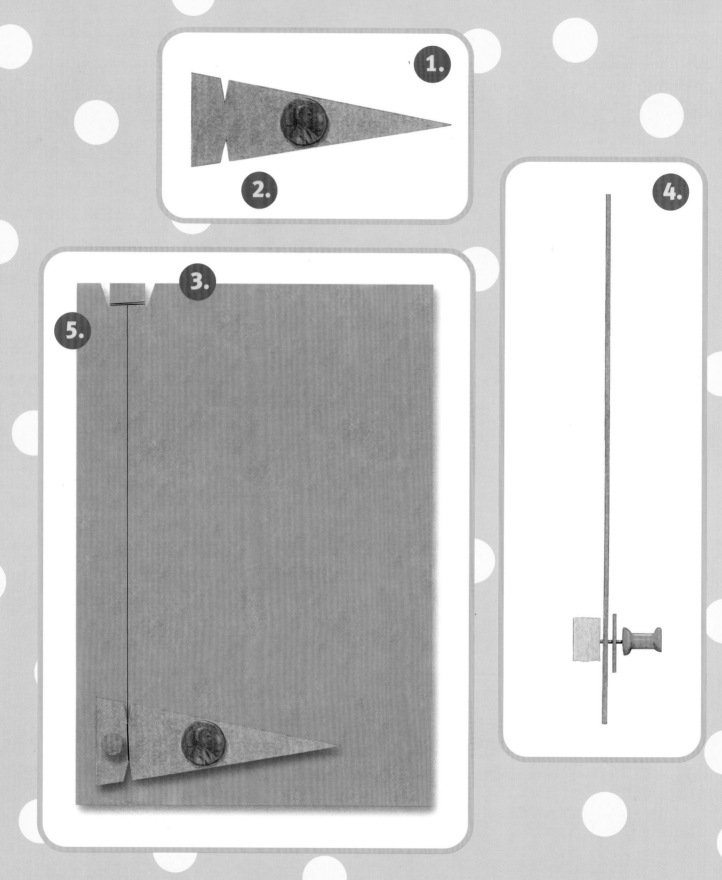

Procedure

1. Using the smaller piece of cardboard, cut a triangular pointer wide enough that the penny will fit on it. Glue the penny in place using Superglue. Cut two small slits into the pointer, as shown opposite.

2. Wrap one end of the strand of hair around the pointer at the slits. Superglue the hair in place.

3. Using the larger piece of cardboard, cut two small slits about half an inch (1.25 cm) apart along one side.

4. Position the pointer on the opposite side of the cardboard from the slits. Use the pushpin to attach the pointer to the large piece of cardboard. Secure the pushpin with the small piece of Styrofoam, as shown below.

5. Pull the opposite end of the strand of hair so that the pointer is horizontal and the hair is stretched to its full length. Wrap the hair around the two slits in the cardboard, making sure that the hair stays stretched. Glue the hair in place at the slits. With a pencil, mark where the pointer is pointing. The completed hair hygrometer should look like the illustration on page 38 (far left).

6. Take a hot shower and bring the hair hygrometer into the bathroom with you. After at least fifteen minutes, use a pencil to mark where the pointer is pointing. This point represents 100 percent humidity.

7. With an adult supervising you, use a hair dryer directly on the strand of hair for two minutes. After that, use a pencil to mark where the pointer is pointing. This point represents 0 percent humidity.

8. Leave your hair hygrometer outside in the shade, someplace where it won't be exposed to rain, snow, or strong winds. Every day, mark where the pointer is pointing, and record the day's humidity (you can check this on the news, in the newspaper, or on the Internet).

Results

Did the hair get shorter or longer at 100 percent humidity in the steamy bathroom? How did the hair's length change when you dried it with the hair dryer? Did the hygrometer change in response to the humidity outside?

Display Tip

Display your hair hygrometer during the science fair. If possible, bring in the hair dryer and show your audience how the hair shrinks at 0 percent humidity.

Extension Question

Does curly hair work better in the hair hygrometer, or is straight hair better? Make two hygrometers, one with a strand of curly hair and one with a strand of straight hair. Do they respond differently to humidity?

Extension Question

How well does damaged hair work in the hair hygrometer? Get a strand of either color-treated or permed hair, build another hygrometer, and repeat your experiments.

Copperplating

An *electrolyte* is a liquid that can easily transfer electrons between metals. By immersing two different metals in an electrolyte, you can cause a thin layer of one metal to be deposited over the other—this is called *immersion plating*. Using an electrolyte such as vinegar, you can transfer electrons between copper wire and an iron nail, and end up with a copperplated nail!

Key words
- Copperplating
- Immersion plating
- Electrolyte

Question
Can metals be transferred using only a liquid solution?

Hypothesis
An electrolyte such as vinegar can transfer electrons from copper to iron. As the copper loses electrons, copper ions are produced, which get dissolved in the electrolyte. Any copper ions that end up near the iron are able to regain electrons to form copper metal. In this way, a thin layer of copper will be deposited over the iron.

Materials
- 10 feet (3 m) of copper wire
- 1 cup (240 mL) of vinegar
- A glass bowl
- An iron nail
- A piece of steel wool

Procedure
1. Wrap the copper wire into a tight coil.

2. Pour the vinegar into the bowl.

3. Scour the iron nail with the steel wool until it is shiny and polished.

4. Place the nail and the coiled copper wire into the bowl.

5. Check for changes in the nail after one hour, two hours, eight hours, and one day.

Results
Did a thin layer of copper get deposited on the nail over time? Did the nail change in color? Did the copper wire get more brittle or dissolve over time? Did you try touching the copper-covered nail? Did the copper coating come off on your finger?

Display Tip
Bring your immersion plating apparatus in to display at the science fair. Copperplate many different metal objects to show your audience.

Extension Question
What happens if you use other combinations of metals? Repeat this experiment using metals such as copper and brass or iron and nickel. Which metal plates on the other?

Extension Question
Does the copper wire dissolve in the electrolyte by itself? Repeat this experiment, but leave the nail out. What does this tell you about how electrons are transferred?

Shiny Penny, Green Penny

A little bit of salt and lemon juice can work wonders on dirty, old pennies—together, they can turn the pennies shiny and bright or dark green. But how can the same ingredients do such different things?

When carrying out this experiment, you may think you are getting different results from doing the same thing—but, in reality, you will see two very different chemical reactions. The dull, dirty coating on old pennies is actually *copper oxide*. When copper oxide reacts with an acid, such as lemon juice, it dissolves, revealing the shiny copper (and copper ions) underneath. As long as the pennies stay submerged and the copper ions do not get exposed to air, the pennies will stay shiny. But if you take the pennies out of the lemon juice and forget to rinse them well to remove all the copper ions, a second chemical reaction can take place between the oxygen in the air and the copper ions. This reaction produces a dark green compound called *malachite*.

Key words
- Ions
- Copper oxide
- Malachite

Question
What will a lemon juice and salt bath do to dull, dirty pennies?

Hypothesis
Pennies treated with lemon juice and salt will react differently depending on whether they are exposed to air or not.

Materials
- 1 cup (240 mL) of lemon juice
- 2 tablespoons (30 mL) of salt
- A bowl
- 10 dull, dirty pennies
- Several paper towels

Procedure
1. Mix the lemon juice and salt in the bowl.

2. Immerse all the pennies in the lemon juice and salt solution.

3. Remove five of the pennies after ten minutes and place them on the paper towels. Do not dry the pennies, and leave them exposed to the air.

4. Examine all ten pennies after one, two, four, and eight hours. Record any changes in color that you notice.

5. After eight hours, remove the immersed pennies from the lemon juice and salt solution and rinse them well under running water.

Results

Did the pennies immersed in the lemon juice and salt solution become shiny and clean? Did the pennies left out on the paper towels acquire a dark green coating? How long did it take for the color changes to occur?

Display Tip

Show your audience what the pennies looked like after the experiment. You may also want to bring in more dirty, old pennies and a lemon juice and salt solution to repeat the experiment during the science fair.

Extension Question

How important is the salt to the results you see? Repeat this experiment with different lemon juice and salt solutions in which the salt concentration varies.

Extension Question

Do other acids produce the same results? Repeat this experiment with orange juice, apple juice, or vinegar instead of lemon juice.

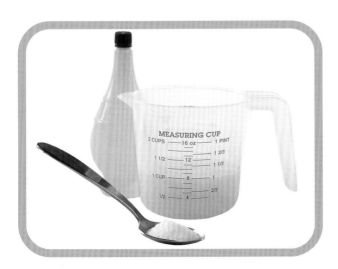

Young and Lovely Vitamin E

Lots of people use beauty creams to stop them from looking older. Have you ever wondered how a cream can be a magic youth solution?

One popular ingredient in anti-aging creams is *vitamin E*. One thing that vitamin E can do is slow chemical processes called *oxidation-reduction reactions* in the cell membranes of the skin. How well does vitamin E work? Test it with this experiment.

Key words
- Vitamin E
- Oxidation-reduction reactions

Question
Can vitamin E slow aging?

Hypothesis
A flower petal coated in vitamin E will stay young and fresh longer than an untreated flower petal.

Materials
- 3 large flower petals (rose petals or orchid petals work well)
- 3 plastic bags
- A marker
- A glass of water
- Several vitamin E capsules

Procedure

1. Place the first flower petal in one of the plastic bags. Using the marker, label this bag "Air."

2. Dip the second flower petal in the water and place it inside another plastic bag. Label this bag "Water."

3. Open the vitamin E capsule and rub the liquid on the third flower petal. Place it inside the last plastic bag and label it "Vitamin E."

4. Observe the flower petals every day for at least three days (continue the experiment longer if you'd like). Record any changes in color, texture, or appearance.

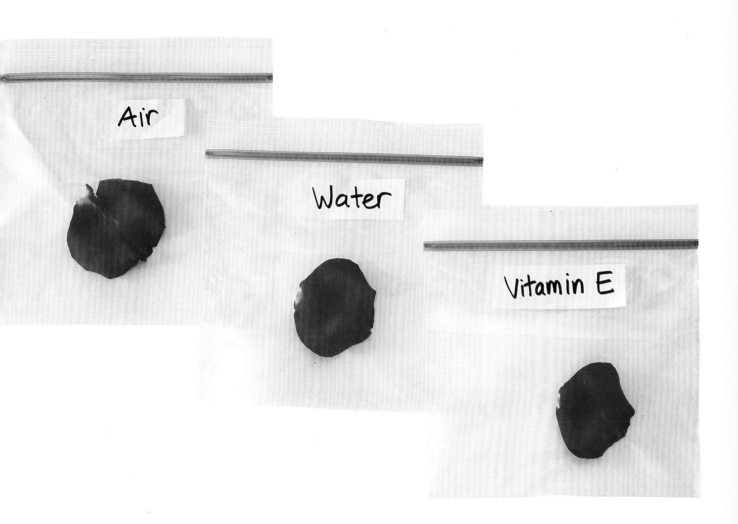

Results

Did the flower petal treated with vitamin E stay fresh the longest? Did the untreated flower petal seem to age most quickly? How did the water affect aging? What does this experiment tell you about how skin ages? Are anti-aging creams useful in helping skin stay more youthful?

Display Tip

Display fresh, dried, and vitamin E–treated flower petals during your presentation so people can see the differences for themselves.

Extension Question

Most manufacturers of beauty creams recommend that people use them every day. Repeat this experiment, reapplying the vitamin E every day to the third flower petal. What happens to its appearance? How long can you keep the flower petal fresh?

Extension Question

What happens if you treat a dried flower petal with vitamin E? Does it become soft and moist again?

Night Stalking

Celery looks like it has tiny straws running up its stalks. These strawlike structures act as tubes to transport nourishment throughout the plant. *Xylem* tubes carry water and *phloem* tubes carry food. The xylem tubes are able to transport water upward through a process called capillary action. Because the xylem tubes of celery are so large, you can watch the *capillary action* take place over time.

Key words
- Xylem
- Phloem
- Capillary action

Question
How is water transported up through a stalk of celery?

Hypothesis
As the red water is drawn up the celery stalk through capillary action, we will be able to see the red color creeping up the stalk.

Materials
- A glass of water (make sure the celery stalk can balance inside the glass, or find a way to prop it up so nothing topples over during the experiment)
- A bottle of red food coloring
- A healthy stalk of celery
- A sunlit windowsill

Procedure
1. Add several drops of food coloring to the water in the glass to give it a bright red color.

2. Position the celery stalk in the glass of red water so it is balanced.

3. Record the time and leave the celery in the red water overnight.

4. In the morning, record the time and examine the celery stalk. Check to see whether any color changes have happened. Measure how far up the stalk the red color has crept.

5. Place the celery stalk back in the red water and place it on the sunlit windowsill. Wait six hours, examine the celery stalk again, and measure how much farther up the red color has crept.

Results
Did the red color slowly creep up the celery stalk? How fast did it move (you can calculate the speed by dividing the inches [cm] of red coloring in the stalk by the number of hours)? Did the color move faster in sunlight than it did overnight?

Display Tip

Bring your brightly colored celery stalk into your presentation to help explain the experiment.

Extension Question

What happens to water as it moves up the celery stalk? Does it mix with water the plant absorbed before or after? Repeat this experiment but add a new color to the water—let the celery sit in red water overnight, and then change it to blue water for a few hours the next morning. Do you see two bands of color, or does the celery stalk turn purple?

Extension Question

Do the xylem tubes exchange water horizontally across different tubes? Cut a 2-inch (5 cm) slit into the base of the celery stalk and place one half of the stalk in red water and the other half in blue water. What happens to the color of the celery?

Soggy Potatoes

A slice of raw potato is usually crisp and firm. The potato cells hold a lot of water, which fills them up and makes them rigid. It is pretty easy to drain the potato cells, though—all it takes is a bit of salt.

Submerging a slice of raw potato in salt water makes the potato cells undergo a process called *osmosis*, where water flows from an area where there is more water to an area where there is less water. Since salt water is less "watery" than the insides of the potato cells, water flows out of the cells, which makes the potato slice soggy and soft.

Key word
Osmosis

Question
What happens to a slice of raw potato in salt water?

Hypothesis
Because of osmosis, placing a raw potato slice in salt water will make water exit the potato cells and leave the slice soft.

Materials
- A marker
- 2 clear plastic cups or drinking glasses, each large enough to hold a potato slice
- 1/2 cup (120 mL) of fresh water
- 1/2 cup (120 mL) of salt water (1 tablespoon [15 mL] of salt dissolved in 1/2 cup [120 mL] of water)
- 2 slices of raw potato, roughly equal in size

Procedure
1. Use the marker to label one drinking glass "Fresh Water" and the other "Salt Water."

2. Fill one glass with fresh water and one glass with salt water, as labeled.

3. Drop one slice of raw potato into each glass. Leave the potato slices overnight.

4. In the morning, examine each potato slice, especially in terms of its texture and consistency.

5. Place the potato slices back into the glasses and leave them for at least another six hours.

6. Examine the slices again after the six hours have passed.

Results

Did the potato slice in fresh water change at all? Did the potato slice in salt water become soggy and soft, and did it get soggier and soggier the longer it sat in the salt water?

Display Tip

This experiment can be displayed during the science fair. You can let your audience handle the two potato slices to show them the differences in texture.

Extension Question

Is the osmosis reversible? Repeat this experiment and submerge the soggy slice in fresh water afterward. Does it go back to normal?

Extension Question

What happens if you use a slice of cooked potato instead of raw potato in this experiment? Does the slice still get soggy in the salt water? Why or why not?

Rubber Chicken

You probably already know that *calcium* helps to keep bones hard and strong. What happens when bones lose calcium? In our bodies, calcium can be lost as we age or if we don't get enough calcium in our diets. To demonstrate the importance of calcium for *bone strength,* you can chemically remove the calcium from a chicken bone, turning it into a rubbery mess. The chemical reaction in this experiment is between the calcium phosphate in the bone and the acetic acid in vinegar. Over time, all the calcium phosphate will dissolve away in the vinegar, and only the protein fibers of the bone will be left.

Key words
- Calcium
- Bone strength

Question
What happens to a bone when it loses calcium?

Hypothesis
Removing the calcium from a chicken bone will leave it rubbery and weak.

Materials
- A marker
- 2 small jars with lids
- Enough water to fill one of the jars
- Enough vinegar to fill one of the jars
- 2 chicken wing bones, cleaned of any meat
- A pair of scissors

Procedure
1. Use the marker to label one jar "Water" and the other "Vinegar."

2. Fill one jar with the water and one jar with the vinegar, as labeled.

3. Drop one chicken bone in each jar. Close the lids on the jars.

4. Leave the bones in the jars for two days.

5. After two days, remove the bones one by one and examine them. Test their flexibility and strength. Record their appearance.

6. Use the scissors to try to cut the bones. Record whether they are easy or difficult to cut.

Results

Was the bone submerged in vinegar rubbery after two days? Was it flexible? Was it glassy or translucent? Did the bone submerged in water change at all after two days? Was the vinegar-dipped bone easy to cut with the scissors? Was the water-dipped bone difficult to cut?

Display Tip

Bring the chicken bones in their water or vinegar jars to the science fair to display. Have your audience examine the differences in the two bones for themselves.

Extension Question

What happens when you leave the rubber bone out in the air to dry? Does it get hard again?

Extension Question

Does this experiment work with other acids, too? Repeat this experiment with lemon juice or apple juice. Does the chicken bone still get rubbery?

Brittle Bones

We know your bones need calcium to be healthy, but calcium alone is not enough to keep them working the way they should. Bones are full of *protein* fibers, which are just as important as calcium for *bone health*.

When you submerge a chicken bone in household bleach, you start a chemical reaction that breaks down most of the proteins and tissues in the bone. All that will be left is the calcium and other minerals—which isn't good for bones!

Key words
• Protein
• Bone health

Question
What happens to a bone when it loses its proteins?

Hypothesis
Removing the proteins and tissues from a chicken bone will leave it brittle.

Materials
• A marker
• 2 small jars with lids
• Enough water to fill one of the jars
• Enough bleach to fill one of the jars
• 3 chicken wing bones, cleaned of any meat
• A pair of tweezers
• A pair of scissors

Safety Warning
Be careful when handling chemicals like bleach, since direct contact can be harmful.

Procedure

1. Use the marker to label one jar "Water" and the other jar "Bleach."

2. Fill one jar with the water and one jar with the bleach, as labeled.

3. Drop one chicken bone in the water jar and two bones in the bleach jar. Close the lids on the jars.

4. Leave the bones in the jars for one day.

5. After one day, use the tweezers to remove one of the bones submerged in bleach. Rinse the bone under running water for two minutes. Examine its appearance and test its strength and flexibility.

6. Remove the bone from the water jar. Examine its appearance and test its strength and flexibility.

7. Use the scissors to try to cut the two bones. Record whether they are easy or difficult to cut.

8. Place the water-submerged bone back in its jar. Wait another day (one bone will still be in the bleach jar).

9. After one more day, remove both remaining bones, using the tweezers to remove the bone from the bleach jar. Again, remember to rinse the bone submerged in bleach under running water for two minutes. Examine the appearance of the bones and test their strength and flexibility. Also, try to cut the bones again.

Results

Were the bones submerged in bleach dry and brittle after one day? Was the remaining bone more so after two days? Did the bone submerged in water change at all after two days? Were the bleach-dipped bones easy to cut with the scissors? Was the water-dipped bone difficult to cut?

Display Tip

Bring the chicken bones in to the science fair to display after you've completed the experiment. Have your audience examine the differences in the bones for themselves.

Extension Question

Bleach is a very strong base. What happens if you use a weaker base. Repeat this experiment, but instead of bleach, use a baking soda solution (2 tablespoons [30 mL] baking soda dissolved in 1 cup [240 mL] of water). How much longer does it take for the chicken bones to become brittle?

Extension Question

Do you think the bleach is breaking down the proteins in the chicken bones by drying them out chemically? Test how a chicken bone dried in the oven (have an adult help you bake the bone for an hour at 400°F) compares to a bleach-dipped bone. Are they both dried out and brittle?

Ocean Pollution

Acid rain is the result of environmental pollution, and it can damage many different life forms. In the ocean, acid rain can weaken the shells of oysters, clams, and mussels. As these organisms die, other animals that normally eat them go hungry. In this way, a little pollution has a great effect.

Calcium, in the form of *calcium carbonate*, is a component of many ocean creatures' shells. When calcium carbonate comes into contact with an acidic substance like acid rain, a chemical reaction takes place, releasing bubbles of carbon dioxide gas. Losing calcium to this chemical reaction makes the ocean creatures' shells more flexible, leaving the creatures within more vulnerable.

You can make this chemical reaction occur at home, using vinegar to take the place of the acid rain.

Key words
- Acid rain
- Calcium carbonate

Question
What does acid pollution do to oyster, clam, and mussel shells?

Hypothesis
Acid pollution (or vinegar) will weaken oyster, clam, and mussel shells, making them more flexible as the calcium is depleted.

Materials
- A marker
- 6 plastic cups
- 2 cleaned oyster shells (available at fish markets)
- 2 cleaned clamshells (available at fish markets)
- 2 cleaned mussel shells (available at fish markets)
- A camera (optional)
- Enough water to fill 3 of the plastic cups
- Enough vinegar to fill 3 of the plastic cups

Procedure

1. Using the marker, label the cups as follows: "Oyster + Water," "Clam + Water," "Mussel + Water," "Oyster + Vinegar," "Clam + Vinegar," and "Mussel + Vinegar."

2. Examine each of the shells before beginning the experiment. Record how hard the shells feel and what they look like. Pay special attention to the shiny surface inside the shells. Take photographs if possible.

3. Place the shells in the correct cups.

4. Add the water to the cups marked "Water" so that the shells are well submerged.

5. Add the vinegar to the cups marked "Vinegar" so that the shells are well submerged.

6. Observe the submerged shells for fifteen minutes. Record anything you notice, especially any bubbling.

7. Examine the submerged shells once a day for three days. Every day, take the shells out one by one and record any changes in appearance, texture, or flexibility. Put them back in the cups and watch for any new bubbling.

Results

Which shells bubbled in the vinegar? What happened over time to the shiny inner surfaces of the shells submerged in vinegar? Did the shells submerged in vinegar feel more flexible as time passed than the shells submerged in water?

Display Tip

It would be great to display the vinegar- and water-soaked shells at the science fair, and also to have fresh shells to submerge in vinegar during your presentation so that the audience can see the bubbling.

Extension Question

Does a little bit of acid hurt the shells as much as a lot of acid? Repeat this experiment using different acids. Use pH paper (from a science supply store) to determine the strength of each acid. Caution When working with strong acids, use rubber gloves and have adult supervision.

Extension Question

Do bases have the same effect on the shells as acids? Repeat this experiment using a baking soda solution (2 tablespoons [30 mL] baking soda dissolved in 1 cup [240 mL] of water) instead of vinegar.

Pollution Catchers

Air pollution is a common problem, especially in cities where cars, congestion, and construction can combine to contaminate the air. Pollutants can cause health problems when people breathe them in on a regular basis. Even in areas where traditional pollution is not so much of a problem, all sorts of other *allergens* (things that cause allergies) can be found in the air. Test the air around you with these pollution catchers and a magnifying glass.

Key word
Allergens

Question
What is really in the air around you, and is all air the same?

Hypothesis
A closer examination will reveal that there are many small particles in air that differ from place to place based on things like pollution and pollen sources.

Materials
- A pair of scissors
- A 4-feet-long (1.2 m) piece of string
- Tape
- 4 white index cards (at least one side must be unlined)
- Enough petroleum jelly to spread a thin layer on one side of each of the index cards
- A plastic zippered bag
- A magnifying glass

Procedure

1. Using the scissors, cut the string into four pieces, each about a foot (30 cm) long. Tape one piece of string to the lined side of each of the index cards to form a loop handle.

2. Smear a thin layer of petroleum jelly on the white side of each index card.

3. Hang three of the index cards in different locations (for example, outside your front door, in the park, and near your school). Hang them in places where they won't be disturbed for two days. Make some notes about the locations, such as whether there is a garden or highway nearby, or whether there is construction being done.

4. Place the last index card inside the plastic zippered bag and leave it untouched for two days.

5. After two days, retrieve all four index cards (remember which card you hung in which location). Use the magnifying glass to examine anything that stuck to the petroleum jelly.

Results

Compared to the card that was placed inside the plastic zippered bag, did the other cards "catch" a lot of particles from the air? Did all the cards look the same? Did some locations seem to have more of one type of pollution (such as pollen in a location near a garden) than others? How clean do you think the air is?

Display Tip

After you've completed the experiment, place each index card in its own plastic zippered bag and label the bags. Display them at the science fair. Bring along your magnifying glass so your audience can take a closer look. Also, prepare a new pollution catcher to hang near your booth at the science fair—show your audience what they are breathing!

Extension Question

Set up pollution catchers around your house, in places such as under the refrigerator, in the fireplace, and under your bed. What kinds of particles do you "catch" in these places?

Extension Question

Repeat this experiment, replacing the pollution catcher every two hours in at least one location. At what time of day is there the most pollution?

Temperature and Transpiration

Plants take up water through their roots and then lose water through structures called *stomata* during a process called *transpiration*. The amount of water a plant loses depends on how often the stomata open to let water out. Environmental conditions can affect the opening of stomata. For example, in a hot, dry climate, such as in the desert, a plant's stomata would often be closed to prevent *dehydration*. You can test the effects of the environment on transpiration with this experiment.

Key words
- Transpiration
- Stomata
- Dehydration

Question
How is transpiration affected by temperature and environment?

Hypothesis
Plants lose more water through transpiration in a cool environment than in a hot, dry one.

Materials
- 2 small plastic soda bottles, cleaned and dried
- Enough water to fill the soda bottles
- A sensitive food scale
- 2 sprouting bean plants with the same number of leaves
- A roll of aluminum foil
- Enough modeling clay to seal the soda bottles
- A desk lamp with a 100-watt bulb

Procedure
1. Fill both of the soda bottles with the water. Weigh them carefully on the food scale and record their weights.

2. Place the roots of one plant into the water in each bottle. Wrap the aluminum foil around the bottom of the plant and the mouth of each bottle to seal it. Complete the seal with a layer of modeling clay to prevent the water from being lost through evaporation.

3. Place one bottle in indirect sunlight.

4. Place the other bottle about a foot (30 cm) from the desk lamp. Position the lamp so the bulb shines directly on the plant. Turn the light on.

5. After three days, remove the plants, aluminum foil, and modeling clay from both bottles. Weigh them carefully on the food scale.

6. Calculate the weight difference between the bottles at the start of the experiment and at the end. This value gives you an idea of how much water each plant used in the three days of the experiment.

Results

Did the plant left under the desk lamp lose less water than the plant in indirect sunlight? Do you think the plant was conserving water because it was in a hot environment?

Display Tip

Bring in one of the bottles with a plant to show your audience what you used to do the experiment. Determine what percentage of the water was used by the plant left in indirect sunlight. Compare it to the percentage used by the plant left under the desk lamp. Make a bar graph to illustrate the difference.

$$\frac{\left(\begin{array}{c}\text{weight of bottle}\\\text{before experiment}\end{array}\right) - \left(\begin{array}{c}\text{weight of bottle}\\\text{after 3 days}\end{array}\right)}{\text{weight of bottle before experiment}} \times 100 = \begin{array}{l}\text{percentage of}\\\text{water used}\end{array}$$

Extension Question

How do you think windy conditions affect transpiration? Repeat this experiment with a plant left near a running table fan instead of a desk lamp.

Extension Question

How do you think humid conditions, such as in a rain forest, affect transpiration? Repeat this experiment with a plant that you mist with water every twenty minutes. Reduce the length of the experiment to six hours instead of three days—or else, you would be sick of misting!

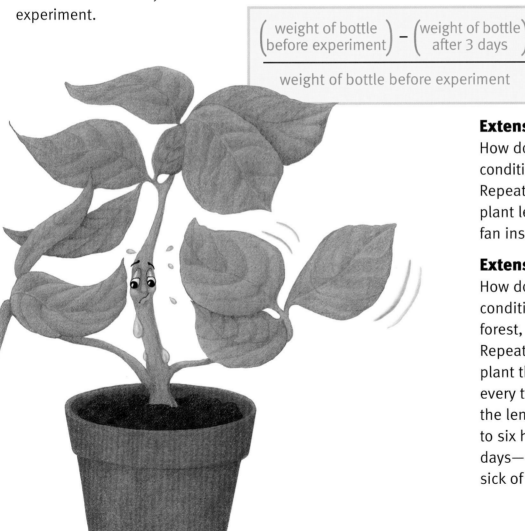

Diaper Secret

The baby diapers that are sold today promise to be super absorbent. Manufacturers can make that claim because most diapers are filled with super water-absorbent polymers. You've probably seen how much liquid these polymers are able to absorb if you've ever seen a diapered baby in a pool—the diaper can literally inflate with water! Explore the properties of these diaper polymers in this experiment.

Key word
Polymers

Question
How much water can diaper polymers absorb? Can the diaper polymers absorb other liquids?

Hypothesis
The polymers inside baby diapers can absorb more than their volume in water. Diaper polymers do not absorb other liquids at the same rate.

Materials
- A pair of scissors
- A disposable diaper
- A measuring spoon
- 4 clear drinking glasses
- A glass of water
- 4 teaspoons (20 mL) of orange juice
- 4 teaspoons (20 mL) of vegetable oil
- 4 teaspoons (20 mL) of milk

Procedure
1. Using the scissors, cut the disposable diaper open over a kitchen counter and remove some of the cottony diaper polymers.

2. Add approximately 2 teaspoons (10 mL) of the polymers to each drinking glass.

3. Add the water to one of the glasses 1 teaspoon (5 mL) at a time, making sure the water gets absorbed. Count how many teaspoons of water can be added before the polymer can't absorb any more.

4. Examine the polymers for any changes in texture or appearance.

5. Add the orange juice, vegetable oil, and milk to the remaining three glasses, one liquid per glass, 1 teaspoon (5 mL) at a time. Examine the polymers in each glass to see if they absorb the different liquids completely.

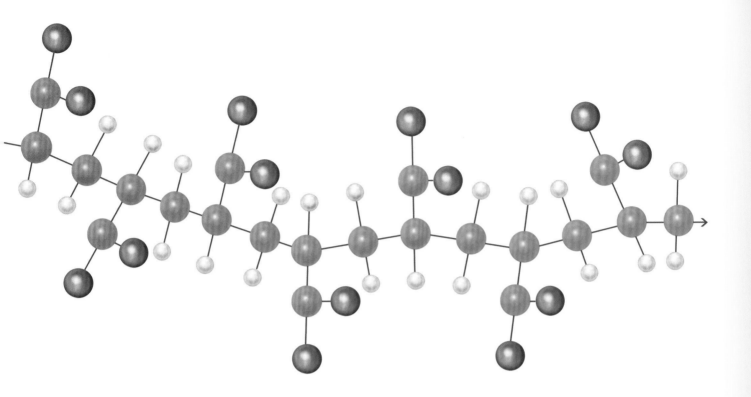

Results

Did 2 teaspoons (10 mL) of the polymer absorb more than 2 teaspoons (10 mL) of water? Did the polymers change in texture after they absorbed the water? Did the polymers absorb the other liquids, either completely or in part?

Display Tip

Bring in a disposable diaper and show your audience what the cottony polymers look like. Put a small amount of the polymer in a cup and add water to it to show your audience how much liquid the polymer can absorb.

Extension Question

Is the absorption reversible—can the polymers be dried out and reused? Add 4 teaspoons (20 mL) of water to 2 teaspoons (10 mL) of polymer. Let the polymers dry for five days. Afterward, add 4 more teaspoons (20 mL) of water. What happens?

Extension Question

Repeat this experiment, but color the water with food coloring. What happens? Do the polymers absorb the dye? What if you let the dyed polymers dry out—does the color evaporate?

24 HOURS
AND COUNTING

Hot Colors

On a hot summer day, you probably see more people wearing white or other light-colored clothing than wearing black or dark-colored clothing. People tend to stay cooler when they wear lighter colors. Have you ever wondered why? A material's color affects how much heat it can absorb—the darker it is, the more its temperature goes up! You can test *heat absorption* by measuring how quickly an ice cube melts when it is covered in dark fabric, compared to an ice cube covered in light fabric.

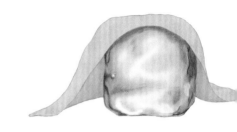

Key word
Heat absorption

Question
Do dark colors absorb more heat than light colors?

Hypothesis
Ice cubes covered in dark-colored fabric will melt more quickly than ice cubes covered in light-colored fabrics.

Materials
- A pair of scissors
- Several fabric samples, at least 6 inches (15 cm) square, of different colors (have at least two light-colored ones, such as white and yellow, and two dark-colored ones, such as black and red)
- 1 ice cube for each fabric sample
- A food scale
- A cookie sheet

Procedure

1. Using the scissors, cut the fabric samples so that they are just slightly larger than the tops of the ice cubes.

2. Weigh the ice cubes to make sure they are all roughly the same size. Record the weights.

3. Place the cookie sheet in direct sunlight.

4. Arrange the ice cubes on the cookie sheet.

5. Cover each ice cube with its own fabric sample.

6. After fifteen minutes, weigh each ice cube again.

Results

Which ice cube melted the most? How did the colors affect the amount the ice cubes melted? What does this tell you about how colors absorb heat?

Display Tip

Determine what percentage of each ice cube melted by subtracting the final weight from the beginning weight, dividing that number by the beginning weight, and multiplying by 100:

$$\frac{(\text{beginning weight} - \text{final weight})}{\text{beginning weight}} \times 100 = \text{percentage melted}$$

Graph these percentages on a bar graph so you can easily display the differences in melting caused by the different fabrics.

Extension Question

What happens if you set up the cookie sheet of ice cubes and fabric samples in the same way, but cover everything with a cardboard box so no light gets in? Do the dark colors still absorb more heat, even without light?

Extension Question

What happens if you set up the cookie sheet of ice cubes and fabric samples in the same way, but place them in the refrigerator instead of in sunlight? Do the dark colors still absorb more heat, even in a cold environment?

You Are a Battery

In a battery, electrons flow between two different metals to create an electrical current. The metals are separated by a fluid, called an *electrolyte*, which can conduct *electrons*. In this experiment, you can build a battery using the sweat on your palms as an electrolyte as you hold two types of metal. This will generate enough current to light a small lightbulb. The electrons will actually travel through your body to complete the electrical circuit!

Key words
- Electrolyte
- Electrons
- Current

Question
Can electricity be conducted through skin?

Hypothesis
Human skin can conduct enough electrical current to light a small lightbulb.

Materials
- A small flashlight bulb
- A bulb holder that will fit your bulb (available at hardware or electrical supply stores)
- 2 electrical lead wires with alligator clips at both ends (available at hardware stores or electrical supply stores)
- A small piece of galvanized steel pipe (available at hardware stores)
- A small piece of copper pipe (available at hardware stores)
- Enough water to wet your hands

Procedure
1. Screw the flashlight bulb into the bulb holder.

2. Attach one alligator clip from one electrical lead wire to one of the terminals on the bulb holder. Attach the other electrical lead wire's alligator clip to the other terminal.

3. Attach one of the free alligator clips to the steel pipe.

4. Attach the last free alligator clip to the copper pipe.

5. Hold the steel pipe tightly in one hand and the copper pipe tightly in the other hand. Watch the lightbulb.

6. Hold the steel pipe tightly with both hands. Watch the lightbulb.

7. Hold the copper pipe tightly with both hands. Watch the lightbulb.

8. Wet your hands. Hold the steel pipe again in one hand and the copper pipe in the other. Watch the lightbulb.

Results
Did the bulb light up when you held both pipes? Did it light up when you held just the steel pipe or just the copper pipe? Did it light up more brightly when your hands were wet?

Display Tip
Have volunteers from your audience try holding the pipes during the science fair.

Extension Question
Repeat this experiment, but this time, you hold one pipe, have a friend hold the other pipe, and then join hands with your friend. What happens? Does the lightbulb still light up?

Extension Question
Replace the lightbulb with an ammeter (available at hardware or electrical supply stores), a device used to measure electrical currents. Repeat this experiment and record how much current each set of conditions creates. How does the amount of current relate to how brightly the lightbulb lit up?

Mini-Lightning

When you see a lightning bolt crashing, it is a great example of how powerful *static electricity* can be. A lightning bolt is made up of a stream of moving electrons leaping through the sky from a cloud to the ground. You can demonstrate the same principles using a piece of Styrofoam and an aluminum pie tin. By rubbing Styrofoam on your hair, electrons get pulled off your hair and piled onto the Styrofoam. When the piled electrons touch the metal pie plate, they jump off, creating a spark.

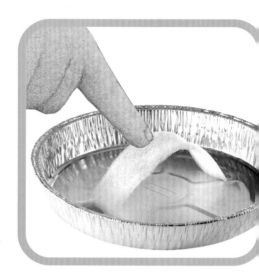

Key word
Static electricity

Question
What conditions cause lightning?

Hypothesis
We can use the properties of Styrofoam to create a pileup of electrons, which can then be discharged in a spark upon contact with metal.

Materials
- A pair of scissors
- A sheet of Styrofoam (from packing materials or the Styrofoam tray that comes from a supermarket bakery) at least as large as the pie tin
- Tape
- An aluminum pie tin
- Another person to turn out the lights

Procedure
1. Using the scissors, cut a strip from the sheet of Styrofoam. Your strip should measure about 1 inch by 4 inches (2.5 x 10 cm).

2. Tape the strip to the inside of the pie tin, like a handle.

3. Rub the rest of the Styrofoam sheet on your hair for one minute. Rub fast, but don't break the sheet!

4. Place the sheet on a table so that the side that you rubbed on your hair faces up.

5. Pick up the pie tin by the handle and hold it about 12 inches (30 cm) over the Styrofoam.

6. Carefully drop the pie tin on the Styrofoam sheet, but don't touch anything yet.

7. Very slowly, touch your finger to the pie tin (don't touch anything else). Do you feel a spark?

8. Use your other hand to grab the handle and have someone else turn off all the lights in the room.

9. Lift up the pie tin and touch your finger to it.

Results
Did you feel a spark when you touched your finger to the pie tin? Did you see a spark when you touched the tin with the lights off? How many times could you touch the pie tin before you couldn't feel or see a spark anymore?

Display Tip

During the science fair, demonstrate the lightning effect to your audience. Invite them to come and try.

Extension Question

Can you transfer electrons to the Styrofoam from materials other than hair? Repeat this experiment, but rub the Styrofoam on silk fabric, paper, glass, and cotton fabric. Which materials cause sparks during the experiment?

Extension Question

Styrofoam is one thing that electrons can pile onto easily; balloons are another. You can rub a balloon on your hair and pile the electrons onto the balloon. Can you design a lightning sparker using a balloon instead of Styrofoam?

Yeast Fermentation

The yeast that is used to bake things such as bread is actually a live *microorganism*. When yeast microbes feed on sugars, they often undergo a process called *fermentation*, which produces energy for the yeast as well as alcohol and carbon dioxide gas as by-products. In a closed container, such as a bottle sealed by a latex balloon, the carbon dioxide gas can be collected as the balloon inflates.

Fermentation is not the only process that yeast microbes use to make energy. In fact, fermentation only occurs when yeast microbes are cut off form a source of oxygen, such as when they are in a closed container. When yeast microbes use oxygen and sugars, they undergo *aerobic respiration*, which also produces energy. During aerobic respiration, however, instead of alcohol being produced, the by-product is water.

Key words
- Microorganism
- Fermentation
- Aerobic respiration

Question
What happens when yeast microbes feed on sugars?

Hypothesis
In a closed container, yeast microbes will undergo fermentation to produce energy. The carbon dioxide made during fermentation can be collected inside an inflating balloon.

Materials
- 2 cups (480 mL) of warm water, measured out in 1-cup (240 mL) portions
- 2 16-ounce water bottles, cleaned and dried
- 2 tablespoons (30 mL) of sugar
- A marker
- 2 packages of active dry yeast
- 2 latex balloons
- Masking tape

Procedure
1. Pour 1 cup (240 mL) of the warm water into each of the two bottles.

2. Add the sugar to one of the bottles and mix well. Using the marker, label this bottle "Sugar Added." Label the other bottle "Control."

3. Add one package of yeast to each bottle and mix well by swirling the bottles.

4. Place a balloon over the mouth of each bottle and tape the balloons into place.

5. Observe what happens to the balloons after five, fifteen, thirty, and sixty minutes. Record your observations.

Results
Did the balloon on the bottle labeled "Sugar Added" inflate? Did it inflate more over time? Did the balloon on the "Control" bottle inflate at all? If so, how did the size of the inflated "Control" balloon compare to the size of the "Sugar Added" balloon? Was the "Control" balloon much smaller?

Bottle	Time (minutes)	Balloon Observations
Control	5	
	15	
	30	
	60	
Sugar Added	5	
	15	
	30	
	60	

Display Tip

Take photographs of the two bottles at each time point to show how the balloons inflated. You could also use a tape measure to determine the girth of each balloon at each time point, and then plot these numbers on a line graph.

Extension Question

How does temperature affect the rate of yeast fermentation? Set up three bottles with yeast and sugar, but use ice-cold water in one, room temperature water in the second, and hot (but not boiling) water in the third. Then repeat steps 4 and 5 of this experiment. Which of the balloons inflates most quickly?

Extension Question

How does the amount of sugar affect yeast fermentation? Set up three bottles with yeast and warm water, but use 1/2 tablespoon (7.5 mL) of sugar in one, 2 tablespoons (30 mL) of sugar in the second, and 5 tablespoons (75 mL) of sugar in the third. Then repeat steps 4 and 5 of this experiment. Which of the balloons inflates most quickly?

Cool Ocean, Hot Land

If you've ever walked along a beach in the summer, you may have noticed that the sand is much warmer than the ocean water, even though the temperature outside is the same for both. Why does one get hotter than the other? The answer has to do with how different substances take up and store heat, a property called *specific heat capacity*. Some materials heat up quickly and cool down quickly, while others take a long time to heat up but also take a long time to cool down.

Key word
Specific heat capacity

Question
Which stores heat more efficiently, the ocean or the beach?

Hypothesis
Even when sand and water are exposed to the same heat source, they will heat up and cool down differently because the two substances have different specific heat capacities.

Materials

- 2 measuring cups, each holding 1 cup (240 mL)
- 1/2 cup (120 mL) of water
- 1/2 cup (120 mL) of sand
- 2 scientific thermometers
- Tape
- A large pot, big enough to hold both measuring cups at once
- Enough water to fill the pot partway
- A stove
- Adult supervision (to heat the pot of water on the stove)
- A timer that measures in seconds

Procedure

1. Add the water to one of the measuring cups and add the sand to the other.

2. Place one thermometer upright in each measuring cup and tape it in place. Let the measuring cups sit for one hour.

3. After one hour, read and record the temperature of the water and sand.

4. Place both measuring cups inside the large pot. Add water to the pot, making sure there isn't enough water for either measuring cup to float.

5. Remove the measuring cups from the pot and place the pot on the stove top.

6. With an adult nearby to supervise, heat the water on the stove top until it is just about to boil. Remove the pot from the heat and place it on a heat-proof surface. This pot of water, or hot-water bath, will be the heat source for the experiment.

7. Place both measuring cups back into the pot. **BE CAREFUL! Don't let your hands touch the hot water.** Turn the timer on. After fifteen seconds, read and record the temperature of the water and the sand.

8. Take the temperature of the water and the sand every thirty seconds for five minutes, recording each value.

9. Remove the measuring cups from the pot and place them on a countertop. **BE CAREFUL! The measuring cups may be hot.**

10. Take the temperature of the water and the sand every thirty seconds for five minutes, recording each value.

Results

Which material heated up more quickly? Which one cooled down more quickly? Was the material that was quick to heat up also the one that was quick to cool down?

Display Tip

Make a graph of the temperature of the water over time and another graph of the temperature of the sand over time to show how slowly or quickly each heated up or cooled down. Using a science textbook or a source online, look up the specific heat capacities of water and sand for your report as well.

Extension Question

The energy source that heats the oceans and beaches of the world is the sun. Energy given out by light is called radiant heat. Repeat this experiment using a source of radiant heat (such as a heat lamp) instead of the hot water bath. Are the results the same? Is one material much better at absorbing radiant heat than the other?

Extension Question

Repeat this experiment, but instead of a hot-water bath, use a cold-water bath by putting ice water instead of hot water in the pot. Are the results the same?

Down the Ramp

Will a heavy cylinder or a light cylinder reach the end of a ramp first? Try this race with a full can of soda and an empty one on a ramp made from a piece of wood propped up by some books. You may think the weight of the full can of soda will make it reach the end of the ramp first, but the heavier something is, the more it is hindered by *friction*—and friction will make the difference in this race.

Key word
Friction

Question
Will the full can or the empty can reach the end of the ramp first?

Hypothesis
Because the full can is heavier, it will be more hindered by friction, and the empty can will win the race.

Materials
- A plank of wood to make a ramp
- A stack of books (or anything that can be used to prop one end of the ramp up)
- A full can of soda
- An empty can of soda

Procedure
1. Make a ramp with the stack of books and the plank of wood.

2. Hold both cans at the top of the ramp.

3. Release the cans.

4. Record which can reaches the bottom of the ramp first.

5. Repeat the race several times to see if one of the cans always wins.

Results

Did the full can seem to be winning the race at the beginning? Did the empty can always win at the end?

Display Tip

Bring your experiment to the science fair and demonstrate the race during your presentation.

Extension Question

Repeat this experiment several times, raising and lowering the ramp each time. Does the winner of the race change when you use a different ramp angle?

Extension Question

Repeat this experiment, but take the ramp outside and coat it in oil (which is a lubricant) to reduce the friction on the cans. Does the empty jar still win the race? Does it win by as much?

Juice Rocket

Lemon juice and baking soda can cause quite a bang! When these two materials mix, a *chemical reaction* occurs that produces carbon dioxide gas. The gas produced exerts pressure, and if the reaction takes place inside a corked bottle, the gas pressure can blow the top right off.

Key word
Chemical reaction

Question
Can lemon juice and baking soda fuel a cork rocket?

Hypothesis
The chemical reaction between lemon juice and baking soda will produce enough carbon dioxide gas to push a cork out of a bottle.

Materials
- 2 tablespoons (30 mL) of baking soda
- A square of toilet paper
- 1/2 cup (120 mL) of lemon juice
- A 16-ounce plastic water bottle, emptied and clean
- A cork that fits snugly into the opening of the water bottle

Procedure

1. Pour the baking soda onto the center of the toilet-paper square. Gather the edges of the square to make a small packet.

2. Add the lemon juice to the water bottle.

3. Drop the baking soda packet into the bottle and quickly seal it with the cork. Make sure the cork is not pointed at anyone.

4. Wait a few minutes and record what happens to the cork.

Results

What happened as the baking soda mixed with the lemon juice? Did you notice any bubbles? Did the cork shoot out as the reaction proceeded?

Display Tip

The science fair coordinators may not want you to demonstrate this experiment during the science fair itself because of the projectile cork, but they may let you show a videotape of the experiment. Make the arrangements in advance.

Extension Question

Lemon juice is an acid and baking soda is a base. The carbon dioxide is produced when the acid and the base mix in a neutralizing reaction. Can you make a rocket with other household acids like vinegar? Which work the best?

Extension Question

The gas produced by the neutralizing reaction can also be collected in a balloon instead of forcing the cork out. Repeat this experiment, but in step 3, replace the cork with a small balloon, taping it tightly around the neck of the water bottle. What happens? Experiment to find out how much baking soda and lemon juice you need to inflate the balloon.

Full of Hot Air

When air inside a closed container is heated, the air molecules begin to move more quickly and exert a *pressure* on the sides of the container. In effect, hot air expands, and when that hot air is enclosed in a flexible container—such as a marshmallow—it can push against the container enough to make the container expand as well.

Key word
Pressure

Question
What happens when you heat a marshmallow?

Hypothesis
Since marshmallows are mostly sugar and water surrounding pockets of air, heating a marshmallow will cause the air pockets inside it to expand and push against the sides of the marshmallow. Since the marshmallow is flexible, it will expand.

Materials
- Adult Supervision
- 4 marshmallows
- 4 paper towels
- A microwave

Procedure
1. Have an adult supervise this experiment, because the marshmallow may get very, very hot.

2. Place the first marshmallow on the first paper towel in the microwave. Heat it on the microwave's highest setting for ten seconds. Take the marshmallow and paper towel out of the microwave. Compare this marshmallow's appearance to the unheated marshmallows.

3. Allow the marshmallow to cool at room temperature. Record how it changes in appearance and texture.

4. Place the second marshmallow on the second paper towel in the microwave. Heat it on the microwave's highest setting for thirty seconds. Take the marshmallow and paper towel out of the microwave. Compare this marshmallow's appearance to the unheated marshmallows.

5. Allow the marshmallow to cool at room temperature. Record how it changes in appearance and texture.

6. Place the third marshmallow on the third paper towel in the microwave. Heat it on the microwave's highest setting for sixty seconds. Take the marshmallow and paper towel out of the microwave. Compare this marshmallow's appearance to the last unheated marshmallow.

7. Allow the marshmallow to cool at room temperature. Record how it changes in appearance and texture.

Results
Did the heated marshmallows expand in size? Which one expanded the most? Did heating the marshmallows for longer cause them to expand more or melt? What happened as the heated marshmallows cooled? Did they return to normal size and shape?

Microwaved Marshmallows

Marshmallow	Time (seconds)	Observations
First	10	
Second	30	
Third	60	

Display Tip

Take photographs of the marshmallows before and after they come out of the microwave, as well as after they've cooled down again. Display your photos at the science fair.

Extension Question

The air inside the marshmallow reacts differently from the sugary parts of the marshmallow to heating and cooling. What happens when you rapidly cool a heated marshmallow? Does the marshmallow cooled in the freezer shrink to the same extent as the marshmallows that cool at room temperature?

Extension Question

Do you think the same principles govern both popcorn popping and the expanding marshmallows? Design an experiment to compare the two processes.

Gelatin Mountains

Static electricity, which is what makes your socks stick to other clothes in the dryer, can be a powerful force. When you rub a piece of wool on a latex balloon, the balloon becomes charged with static electricity. If you hold the charged balloon near a pile of unflavored gelatin, the gelatin becomes charged as well, but with the opposite charge. Things that have opposite charges attract, so the gelatin starts to creep toward the balloon, trying to make contact.

lime gelatin

baking soda

Key word
Static electricity

Question
What happens to unflavored gelatin when it is placed near a charged object?

Hypothesis
Bringing a charged balloon near a plate of unflavored gelatin powder will charge the powder and attract it toward the balloon.

Materials
- 3 tablespoons (45 mL) of unflavored powdered gelatin
- A paper plate
- A latex balloon, inflated
- A woolen sweater

Procedure
1. Sprinkle the unflavored powdered gelatin on the paper plate.

2. Rub the latex balloon on the woolen sweater for thirty seconds.

3. Hold the balloon so that the part that was rubbed against the sweater is directly above the gelatin on the paper plate.

4. Slowly lower the balloon until it is about an inch (2.5 cm) above the gelatin. Don't let the balloon and the gelatin touch.

5. After ten seconds, begin to slowly raise the balloon. Observe what happens to the gelatin.

Results
Was the gelatin attracted to the charged balloon? Did it seem to form peaks like a mountain? How high did the gelatin mountain rise?

Display Tip
You can repeat this entire experiment during the science fair, but have photographs of all of the steps to display, too, just in case something goes wrong with the demonstration!

Extension Question
Repeat this experiment using flavored gelatin (which has sugar added) instead of unflavored gelatin. What happens? Do you see the same results?

Extension Question
Repeat this experiment using powdered sugar, salt, baking soda, or baby powder instead of unflavored gelatin. What happens? Which of these substances gives you the highest mountains?

Raisin Dance

Drop some raisins into a glass of club soda and watch them magically dance around! Actually, there's no magic here—the raisins fall down because they are denser than the club soda, but when bubbles from the soda attach to the raisins, the *buoyancy* of the raisins changes. With enough attached bubbles, a raisin can actually float—until, of course, the bubbles float off.

Key word
Buoyancy

Question
Can raisins both float and sink in a glass of club soda?

Hypothesis
The bubbles in club soda can attach to raisins and change their buoyancy.

Materials
• A clear drinking glass
• Club soda (make sure it's not flat)
• 6 raisins, cut in half

Procedure
1. Fill the glass with club soda.

2. Drop the raisin halves into the glass.

3. Observe what happens to the raisins.

Results
Did the raisins float or sink? Did bubbles attach to the raisins? What caused a floating raisin to begin to sink? What caused a sinking raisin to begin to float?

Display Tip
During the science fair, have a glass of dancing raisins on display. Let your audience drop raisin halves into the club soda to make them dance.

Extension Question

The wrinkles in the raisins make it easy for bubbles to attach. Does this experiment work with things that have similar weights but different textures? Try this experiment with chocolate chips, nuts, or small beads. Which ones dance?

Extension Question

How big can the raisin pieces be and still work in this experiment? Try different sizes of raisin pieces. Which size makes the best dancers?

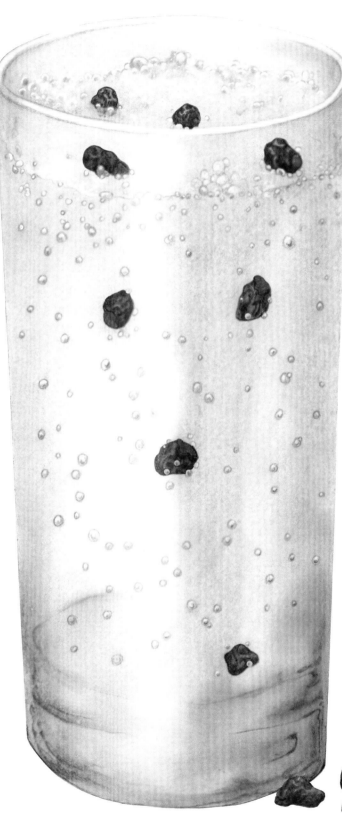

Levitation

Airplanes are heavier than air, but they manage to fly. Have you ever wondered why? According to *Bernoulli's Principle*, objects such as airplanes can float if the air pressure beneath them is greater than the air pressure above them. For airplanes, the air rushing over the wings doesn't push down on the plane as much as the air from underneath pushes up. This creates an upward force, or *lift*. In the case of a table tennis ball in a stream of air from a hair dryer, the moving stream of air exerts less pressure on the ball than the stationary air in the room around it. Because of this, the ball will stay floating in the stream of moving air rather than falling out of it.

Key words
- Bernoulli's Principle
- Lift

Question
How can we use a stream of air to cause something to levitate?

Hypothesis
The air pressure created by a stream of air can hold up a table tennis ball.

Materials
- A hair dryer
- A table tennis ball

Procedure
1. Turn the hair dryer on (if it has a cool air setting, use that) and point it straight up.

2. Balance the table tennis ball above the air stream from the hair dryer, experimenting with its position until you find a spot where the ball levitates in midair.

3. Pull the ball slightly out of the air stream and let it go. What happens?

4. Slowly move the hair dryer from side to side, observing what happens to the ball.

Results

Did the table tennis ball levitate? Did the ball get sucked back into the air stream when you pulled it out slightly? Did the ball move with the stream of air when you moved the hair dryer?

Extension Question

What other things can you levitate with the hair dryer? Repeat this experiment using a toilet-paper roll, a cookie, and a paper clip instead of the table tennis ball. How do you think the shape of an object affects the amount of lift generated?

Extension Question

Can you levitate more than one object at the same time? Experiment with different combinations.

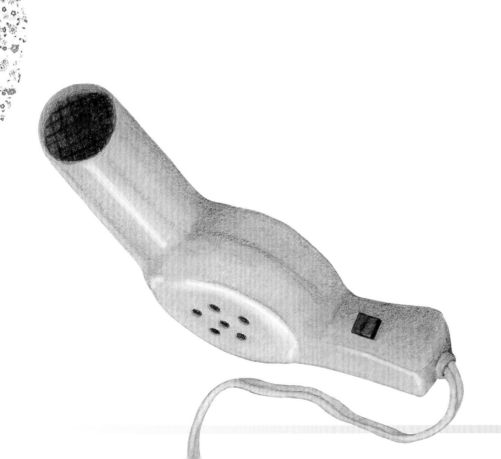

Spud Power

Potatoes are yummy, but they are also electric! Potatoes contain *phosphoric acid*, which can be used as an *electrolyte* to make a battery. All you have to do is provide two *electrodes* (a penny and a galvanized nail will work), some wiring, and a small lightbulb.

The phosphoric acid in the potato starts a chemical reaction between the copper in the penny and the iron in the nail. Electrons begin to flow, creating an electrical current that flows through the wires and lights the bulb.

Key words
- Phosphoric acid
- Electrolyte
- Electrode

Question
Can you make a battery out of a potato?

Hypothesis
The acid inside a potato can act as an electrolyte and conduct electricity; therefore, a potato can be used as a battery to power a small lightbulb.

Materials
- A small flashlight bulb
- A bulb holder that will fit your bulb
- 2 electrical lead wires with alligator clips at both ends (available at hardware stores)
- A knife and an adult's help
- A potato
- A penny
- A galvanized nail

Procedure
1. Screw the flashlight bulb into the bulb holder.

2. Attach one electrical lead wire to each of the terminals on the bulb holder. Make sure you use two different wires!

3. Using the knife, have an adult help you cut two small slits in the potato. Make sure the slits are at least an inch (2.5 cm) apart. Insert the penny into one slit and the nail into the other.

4. Attach one of the free alligator clips to the nail.

5. Attach the other free alligator clip to the penny.

6. Watch the lightbulb.

Results
When all the wires were connected, did the bulb light up?

Display Tip
Have your potato battery ready to use at the science fair. Show your spud power by lighting up the flashlight bulb for your audience.

Extension Question
What happens if you connect many potato batteries in series? Assemble three potato batteries and line them up on the table, right to left. Attach an electrical lead wire to the bulb and the penny on the far right potato. Attach another electrical lead wire to the bulb and the nail on the far left potato. Attach two more electrical lead wires between (1) the nail on the far right potato and the penny on the middle potato and (2) the nail on the middle potato and the penny on the far left potato. Does the bulb light up more brightly? Do you think you've created a stronger battery?

Extension Question
Other fruits and vegetables can make great batteries, too. Repeat this experiment using a lemon, an orange, a tomato, or a squash instead of the potato. Which works best?

Underwater Fireworks

This experiment isn't really about fireworks, but the burst of color you will create will look a lot like fireworks. Using a bit of food coloring and oil, you can create firework-like effects in a tall glass of water. The bursts happen because of how food coloring wants to react when it comes into contact with water.

If you've ever dropped a bit of food coloring into water, you've noticed that the color begins to spread almost immediately. This spreading process is called *diffusion*. On the other hand, if you've ever dropped a bit of oil into water, you've noticed that the oil never mixes with the water—the two liquids are *immiscible*. In this experiment, by mixing the food coloring with oil before you drop it in the water, you give the food coloring a waterproof shield—for a moment. As the oil and food coloring shift against each other, the food coloring eventually finds a hole in the shield and comes into contact with the water. Then, the color comes bursting out!

Key words
- Diffusion
- Immiscible

Question
How is diffusion affected when one of the liquids is mixed with an immiscible substance?

Hypothesis
Mixing food coloring with oil and then dropping the mixture into water will initially prevent diffusion. At some point, however, the food coloring will come into contact with the water and the color will quickly diffuse.

Materials
- A spoon
- 1 tablespoon (15 mL) of food coloring
- 1 tablespoon (15 mL) of cooking oil
- A small mixing bowl
- A medicine dropper
- A large clear glass jar filled with water

Procedure

1. Using the spoon, mix the food coloring and oil in the bowl.

2. Fill the medicine dropper with the mixture of food coloring and oil.

3. Dip the tip of the medicine dropper under the water level in the jar.

4. Release one drop of the food coloring–oil mixture into the water.

5. Observe what happens to the color.

6. Repeat the experiment to confirm your observations.

Results

What happened to the color under the water? How quickly did the color diffuse? What happened to the oil?

Display Tip

Have a jar, lots of fresh water, the mixture of food coloring and oil, and a medicine dropper on hand at the science fair. Let your audience make fireworks of their own!

Extension Question

What happens if you reverse the oil and water? Repeat the experiment, filling the jar with oil and mixing the food coloring with 1 tablespoon (15 mL) of water. Do you still see a firework display?

Extension Question

What happens if you mix some alcohol with the water? Prepare a solution of water and rubbing alcohol by combining 1/2 cup (120 mL) of water with 1/2 cup (120 mL) of alcohol. Repeat this experiment using the water-alcohol solution instead of plain water. Alcohol is able to dissolve water and oil. Do you still see underwater fireworks?

Carton Turbine

A *turbine* is a kind of machine that rotates. Often turbines are powered by steam, gas, or wind. This turbine will turn powered by water and gravity.

As the water rushes out of the holes of the milk carton, it exerts a force that pushes the carton in a certain direction. This happens because of one of *Newton's laws of motion* Every action has an equal and opposite reaction. When four reactions combine, as in this experiment, the results will leave you — and the carton — spinning.

Key words
- Turbine
- Newton's laws of motion

Question
What happens when water flows out of four small holes in a hanging carton?

Hypothesis
If the holes on the carton are positioned with one on each side, the forces generated by the flowing water will spin the carton.

Materials
- A half-gallon milk container, cleaned and dried
- A nail to poke holes in the milk carton
- A piece of string about 4 feet (1.2 m) long
- A place outside to do the experiment
- A bucket
- Enough water to fill the bucket
- An assistant (this isn't necessary, but it will make things easier)

Procedure
1. Use the nail to poke a hole in the bottom right corner of each of the four faces of the milk carton.

2. Poke another hole through the top of the milk carton. Tie the string through that hole.

3. Hang the carton by the string to a tree branch or something similar outside. Make sure it is low enough that you have access to the top of the carton.

4. Fill the bucket with the water and take it over to the carton.

5. If you have an assistant helping you, have him or her hold fingers over the four holes on the faces of the milk carton as you pour water from the bucket into the carton. When the carton is full, have your assistant remove his or her fingers and step away from the carton.

6. Observe what happens.

Results

Did the carton begin to spin as the water flowed out? Did it spin clockwise or counterclockwise?

Display Tip

This experiment is too messy to demonstrate during the science fair. Instead, you could arrange to play a short videotape of the experiment. If that isn't possible, take lots of photographs!

Extension Question

Repeat this experiment, but poke the holes in the bottom left corners of each of the four faces of the milk carton instead. What happens? Does the carton turbine spin the other way?

Extension Question

Repeat this experiment, but poke the four holes in four different parts of the carton (the bottom right corner of one face, the bottom left corner of the second, the bottom center of the third, and the top center of the last face). What happens? Does the carton spin?

Glue-y Gooey Slime

Polymers are special compounds made of long chains of molecules. They are often rubbery and stringy—rubber bands are a good example of polymers in action. You can make polymers at home using some simple ingredients. Have some gooey fun with glue!

Key word
Polymer

Question
What happens when you mix glue with Borax?

Hypothesis
Mixing glue with Borax will yield a polymer that will have different properties than either of the starting materials.

Materials
- 2 mixing bowls
- 1/2 cup (120 mL) of water
- 1/2 tablespoon (7.5 mL) of Borax detergent
- 3 mixing spoons
- 3 tablespoons (45 mL) of water
- 6 tablespoons (90 mL) of Elmer's® glue
- A measuring spoon

Procedure

1. In one of the mixing bowls, combine the 1/2 cup (120 mL) of water and the Borax. Using the first mixing spoon, mix well.

2. In the other mixing bowl, combine the 3 tablespoons (45 mL) of water with the glue. Using the second mixing spoon, mix well.

3. Measure out 3 tablespoons (45 mL) of the Borax-water mixture and add it to the watered-down glue. Using the third spoon, mix well for two minutes.

4. After two minutes, examine the texture of the glue-Borax-water mixture.

Results

Was the glue-Borax-water mixture a different texture than the glue by itself? Is it more stringy and rubbery? Did it lose its stickiness?

Display Tip

Have a batch of glue-y gooey slime ready to display at the science fair.

Extension Question

Let a dollop of glue dry and a blob of glue-y gooey slime dry. How do the two compare?

Extension Question

Another way to make slime is to use liquid starch instead of Borax. Repeat this experiment using liquid starch in place of the Borax-water mixture. How does this slime compare to the Borax version?

Mini-Rocket

Combining chemistry and physics can give you an explosive effect. For example, when an antacid tablet is dissolved in water, a *chemical reaction* takes place to produce carbon dioxide gas (that's why antacid tablets fizz). All that extra gas released by the reaction has to go somewhere—and if it is enclosed in a tight space (such as a closed film canister), it creates a lot of *pressure*.

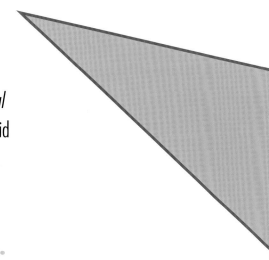

Key words
- Chemical reaction
- Pressure

Question
What happens when an antacid tablet is dissolved in water in a closed container?

Hypothesis
The gas produced when an antacid tablet dissolves in water creates enough pressure to shoot a closed film canister into the air.

Materials
- A spot outside to conduct the experiment
- 1 teaspoon (5 mL) of water
- An antacid tablet
- A canister from a 35-mm roll of film, including the lid

Procedure
1. Find a spot outside, far from cars or other children, to conduct this experiment.

2. Add the water and antacid tablet to the canister and quickly replace the lid on the canister, making sure it is on tight.

3. Quickly place the canister on the ground, cap side down, and move about 6 feet (1.8 m) away.

4. Observe what happens after about ten seconds.

5. If nothing happens within one minute, examine the canister. The lid was probably not on tightly enough. You can clean out the canister and try again.

Results
Did the canister shoot up into the air like a rocket? Did you hear a popping sound?

Display Tip
Though you cannot demonstrate this rocket indoors, you can bring antacid tablets to the science fair and dissolve them in cups of water to show your audience the fizzing that takes place.

Extension Question
What happens if you repeat this experiment but place the canister on the ground cap side up? Does the cap fly off?

Extension Question
Does the rocket fly better if you add fins and a nose cone? Repeat this experiment, making the fins and nose cone out of paper and taping or gluing them to the canister. Do the fins and nose cone change the aerodynamics of the rocket?

How Much Vitamin C?

It is important to get enough vitamin C in your diet. But which juices give you the most vitamin C? And do vitamin-fortified juices really give you more for your money? By using a chemical reaction that changes color when there is a certain concentration of vitamin C, you can rank the vitamin C content of different juices.

When iodine is mixed with a starch solution, it turns a deep purple-blue color. When enough vitamin C is added, the purple-blue color disappears. The lower the amount of juice required to make the purple-blue color disappear, the more vitamin C there is in that juice.

Key word
Vitamin C

Question
Can you use chemistry to determine the amount of vitamin C in juice?

Hypothesis
The higher the concentration of vitamin C, the lower the amount of juice needed to clear the purple-blue color of the iodine-starch solution.

Materials
- A mixing bowl
- 2 tablespoons (30 mL) of cornstarch
- 1 cup (240 mL) of water
- A spoon (to mix the cornstarch and water)
- 4 drops of iodine solution
- A measuring spoon
- 6 clear drinking glasses
- A few ounces each of 6 different types of juice, including at least one that claims to be vitamin C–fortified
- A medicine dropper

Safety Warning
Be careful when handling chemicals such as iodine, since direct contact can be harmful.

Procedure

1. In the mixing bowl, combine the cornstarch and water. Using the spoon, mix well to dissolve all the cornstarch.

2. Add the iodine solution to the bowl one drop at a time until the liquid in the bowl turns a dark purple-blue color.

3. Measure out 2 tablespoons (30 mL) of the cornstarch-iodine solution into each of the six drinking glasses.

4. Add the first juice sample to the first glass, one drop at a time. Gently swirl the liquid in the glass after every few drops. Count and record how many drops of juice it takes to clear the purple-blue color.

5. Repeat the previous step for each of your juice samples using one glass per sample.

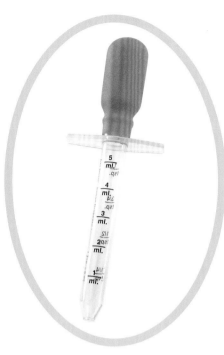

Results

How much of each juice juice did it take to clear the purple-blue color of the cornstarch-iodine solution? Did it take less vitamin C–fortified juice to clear the color?

Display Tip

You could demonstrate the color-change reaction between the iodine-cornstarch solution and vitamin C by having one sample for your science fair demonstration.

Extension Question

Is there vitamin C in other foods as well? Repeat this experiment using milk, tomato juice, tea, coffee, or soda instead of juice. What are your results?

Extension Question

Does this experiment only work for liquids? Can you think of a way to test solid foods for vitamin C using this setup?

Into (Mostly) Thin Air

Every year, the United States uses 200 million cubic feet (5.7 million cubic meters) of Styrofoam packing peanuts. When you consider that the interior volume of the Metrodome in Minneapolis, Minnesota is 60 million cubic feet (1.7 million cubic meters), you can get an idea of just how much Styrofoam that is. What do we do with all this used Styrofoam?

One advantage of Styrofoam packing peanuts is that they can be reused. Your parents have probably packed boxes using packing peanuts they received in other packages. As it turns out, packing peanuts are also made up mostly of air, which means that dissolving them might be a way to reduce their volume.

Key word
Styrofoam

Question
Can Styrofoam packing peanuts be dissolved to reduce their volume?

Hypothesis
Because packing peanuts are made mostly of air, breaking down the Styrofoam with a solvent like acetone will dramatically reduce their volume.

Materials
- A glass jar or glass measuring cup
- Enough acetone nail polish remover to fill the bottom inch (2.5 cm) of the jar
- Styrofoam packing peanuts

Procedure

1. Pour the nail polish remover into the jar.

2. Drop the packing peanuts one by one into the jar. Observe what happens to them.

Results

Did the packing peanuts seem to dissolve away into thin air? Was there any debris left over in the jar after the packing peanuts dissolved?

Display Tip

Check whether you may bring acetone nail polish to the science fair. If so, have your materials ready to demonstrate this experiment to the audience.

Extension Question

What other solvents can dissolve packing peanuts? Repeat this experiment, but replace the nail polish remover with water, vinegar, rubbing alcohol, or bleach.

Extension Question

Since packing peanuts are mostly air, how much can they be compacted by crushing? If you have a trash compactor, have an adult help you use it to compact packing peanuts. How much of a volume reduction can you get?

Vampire Suds

The world is full of acids and bases. Lemon juice is an *acid;* bleach is a *base;* vinegar is an acid; baking soda is a base—the list goes on and on. Some chemicals can tell us whether a particular substance is acidic or basic. These chemicals are called *indicators,* and they often change colors in the presence of an acid or base.

A mixture of turmeric and rubbing alcohol can act as an indicator—can you figure out the color change it undergoes?

Procedure

1. Using the spoon, mix the turmeric and alcohol in the bowl.

2. Dip the bar of soap in the turmeric-alcohol mixture. Record any color changes that occur.

3. Take the soap out of the turmeric-alcohol mixture. Record any changes in the appearance of the turmeric-alcohol mixture or the soap.

Key words
- Acid
- Base
- Indicator

Question
What happens when a turmeric-alcohol mixture comes into contact with soap (a base)?

Hypothesis
A turmeric-alcohol mixture will change color to indicate the presence of a base.

Materials
- 1/2 teaspoon (2.5 mL) of turmeric (a spice available at a grocery store)
- 1/2 cup (120 mL) of rubbing alcohol
- A bowl
- A bar of soap

Results
What color was the turmeric-alcohol mixture at the start of the experiment? What color did the mixture turn when you dipped the soap into it? Did it turn red? Did the soap remain red when you took it out of the turmeric-alcohol mixture?

Display Tip

Bring the materials for this experiment to the science fair. Demonstrate the experiment to your audience. Let the judges drop the soap into the turmeric-alcohol indicator.

Extension Question

Does the turmeric-alcohol indicator return to its original color if you add acid? Repeat this experiment adding vinegar, 1 teaspoon (5 mL) at a time, to the turmeric-alcohol indicator after it has turned red.

Extension Question

What other substances turn the turmeric-alcohol indicator red? Repeat this experiment using other household products, such as orange juice, maple syrup, laundry detergent, or body lotion instead of soap.

How Cold!

Chemistry can be pretty cold. An *endothermic reaction* is one that has to absorb energy, usually in the form of heat, in order to proceed. This means that the temperature of the reaction drops. When the citric acid in lemon juice reacts with baking soda, the reaction can really cool things down.

Key word
Endothermic reaction

Question
What happens when lemon juice reacts with baking soda?

Hypothesis
When citric acid and baking soda react, an endothermic reaction occurs.

Materials
- 1/2 cup (120 mL) of room-temperature lemon juice
- A Styrofoam cup
- A thermometer that fits inside the cup
- 1 teaspoon (5 mL) of baking soda
- A spoon for stirring
- A stopwatch or timer

Procedure
1. Add the lemon juice to the cup.

2. Place the thermometer in the cup. After five minutes, read the thermometer and record the temperature of the lemon juice.

3. Remove the thermometer.

4. Add the baking soda to the cup and stir with the spoon.

5. Replace the thermometer in the cup.

6. After one minute, read the thermometer and compare this reading to the first reading.

7. Take additional temperature readings at two, five, and ten minutes.

Results
Did the mixture in the cup get colder as time went on? Did you see bubbles form in the cup (carbon dioxide gas is one of the by-products of this reaction)?

Display Tip
You can repeat this entire experiment during the science fair. Let your audience watch the thermometer as the temperature drops.

Extension Question
Repeat this experiment, but double the amount of baking soda. What happens? Does the reaction stay cold longer? Is there more fizzing?

Extension Question
Repeat this experiment, but use cold lemon juice instead of room-temperature lemon juice. What happens? Does the baking soda mix as easily?

How cool is this?!

Cup contents	Time	Temperature readings
Lemon juice	5 minutes	
Lemon juice and baking soda	1 minute	
	2 minutes	
	5 minutes	
	10 minutes	

How Hot!

Chemistry can be pretty hot, too! An *exothermic reaction* is one that releases energy in the form of heat. When vinegar reacts with steel wool, it can chemically remove the protective coating on the steel wool, allowing it to rust. During the rusting reaction, iron combines with oxygen in the air. Is this a "hot" reaction? Find out!

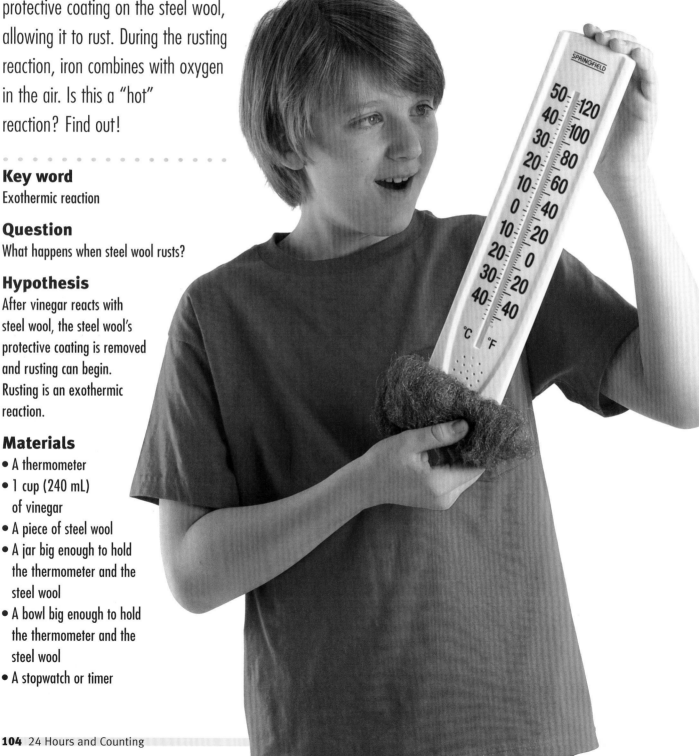

Key word
Exothermic reaction

Question
What happens when steel wool rusts?

Hypothesis
After vinegar reacts with steel wool, the steel wool's protective coating is removed and rusting can begin. Rusting is an exothermic reaction.

Materials
- A thermometer
- 1 cup (240 mL) of vinegar
- A piece of steel wool
- A jar big enough to hold the thermometer and the steel wool
- A bowl big enough to hold the thermometer and the steel wool
- A stopwatch or timer

Procedure

1. Place the thermometer in the jar and close the lid.

2. After five minutes, read the thermometer and record the temperature inside the jar.

3. Pour the vinegar into the bowl.

4. Soak the steel wool in the vinegar.

5. After two minutes, remove the steel wool and squeeze out the excess vinegar.

6. Wrap the steel wool tightly around the thermometer.

7. Place the thermometer and steel wool inside the jar and close the lid.

8. After five minutes, read the thermometer and compare this reading with the first reading.

Before the vinegar · *After the vinegar*

Results

Did the steel wool get hotter after it had been dipped in vinegar? Could you see rust beginning to form?

Display Tip

Make a bar graph of the temperature readings to show what happened during the reaction.

Extension Question

Do you get an exothermic reaction if you use other acids besides vinegar? Repeat this experiment using lemon juice instead of vinegar. What happens?

Extension Question

What happens if you use a base instead of an acid? Repeat this experiment, but instead of vinegar, use a baking soda solution (2 tablespoons [30 mL] baking soda dissolved in 1 cup [240 mL] of water). Does a reaction happen? Does the temperature of the reaction change at all?

Speedy Stalactites

In a cave, mineral-rich water drips down slowly. As the water is exposed to air, it evaporates, and the resulting solution becomes supersaturated. Eventually, mineral crystals begin to form and deposit. These mineral structures are called *stalactites* (when they hang from the cave's roof or sides) or *stalagmites* (when they form on the cave floor).

This experiment will re-create this process, but you will use a supersaturated solution of Epsom salts instead of the mineral solutions found in caves. Your stalactites will grow in a few hours, whereas real ones can take years.

Key words
- Crystal
- Supersaturated solution
- Stalactite
- Stalagmite

Question
How do stalactites form?

Hypothesis
By using an Epsom salt solution, you can model the formation of stalactites (and maybe stalagmites).

Materials
- 1 cup (240 mL) of hot water
- 2/3 cup (160 mL) of Epsom salts
- 2 drinking glasses, each large enough to hold half the Epsom salt solution
- A piece of cardboard, 4 inches (10 cm) square
- A mixing bowl
- A spoon (to mix the Epsom salt and water)
- A piece of wool yarn, about 18 inches (45 cm) long
- 2 paper clips

Procedure

1. Set up the glasses and the cardboard so that the cardboard is in the middle and the drinking glasses are on either side.

2. Using the spoon, mix the hot water and the Epsom salts in the bowl until everything has dissolved.

3. Attach one of the paper clips to each end of the piece of yarn.

4. Dip the yarn in the Epsom salt solution.

5. Pour the Epsom salt solution into the drinking glasses.

6. Hang the yarn across the glasses so that the paper clip ends are submerged in the Epsom salt solution and the middle of the piece of yarn sags over the cardboard.

7. Observe the string over the next few hours. Let the stalactites grow for at least twenty-four hours, but the longer you can leave them growing, the better.

Results

Did a stalactite that hung down from the yarn begin to form? Did it grow over time? Did a stalagmite form on the cardboard?

Display Tip

Take plenty of photographs of the stalactite as it forms, making sure to note how much time has passed for each photo. If you transport it carefully, you may be able to display the stalactite at the science fair.

Extension Question

Repeat this experiment, but use an unsaturated solution of Epsom salts (1/4 cup [60 mL] of Epsom salts in 1 cup [240 mL] of hot water) in step 2. Do stalactites still form? Does it take longer?

Extension Question

Repeat this experiment using table salt instead of Epsom salts in step 2. Do stalactites form as quickly? Do they look the same as the Epsom salt stalactites?

Index

About the Author

Sudipta completed two biology degrees at the California Institute of Technology and spent many years enjoying the sunshine of SoCal. After all that time in L.A., it was hard to return to the frozen wasteland that is the East Coast, but Sudipta eventually found herself at home back East. She now lives in New Jersey with her husband and children.

Sudipta is the author of several books for children. Her upcoming science titles include books in a new series called *The Mad Scientist's Library*. In her free time, she enjoys reading, gossiping over hot chocolate, shopping for shoes, and sleeping in.